EXTREME SCIENCE EXPERIMENTS

ANNA CLAYBOURNE

ARCTURUS

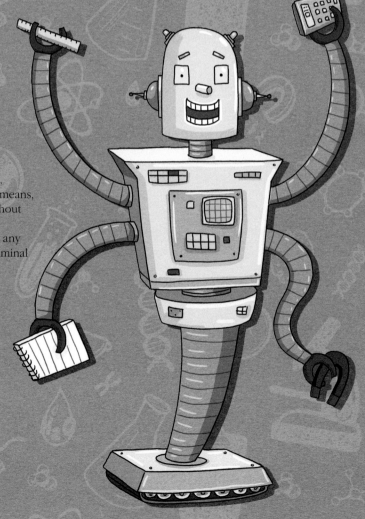

ARCTURUS

This edition published in 2018 by Arcturus Publishing Limited
26/27 Bickels Yard, 151–153 Bermondsey Street,
London SE1 3HA

Author: Anna Claybourne
Science consultant: Thomas Canavan
Experiment illustrations: Jessica Secheret
Other illustrations: Richard Watson
Photos: Shutterstock
Design: Supriya Sahai
Editor: Joe Fullman

ISBN: 978-1-78428-806-8
CH005736US

Supplier 26, Date 1117, Print run 5982

Printed in China

CONTENTS

START EXPERIMENTING!

This book is packed with exciting experiments that go bang, make a big splat, or are so incredible you won't believe your eyes! But there's nothing magical in these pages—it's all real-life amazing SCIENCE.

WHAT YOU'LL NEED

You can do most of these experiments with everyday items you'll find around the house, or can buy easily and cheaply at a supermarket or hardware store.

Some useful things to have handy are ...

* Paper and cardboard
* Pens and pencils
* String
* Glue
* Tape
* Straws (plastic ones are best)
* Plates, bowls, jugs, and plastic food containers
* Scissors
* Paper cups
* Balloons

STAY SAFE!

Experiments are fun, but some of them can be dangerous if they're not done carefully ... so don't forget these safety tips:

✱ You will need an adult to help with experiments that involve cooking and heating, matches and candles, and sharp cutting tools. Wherever an experiment has something like this in it, you'll see this sign to remind you:

⚠ **ASK AN ADULT!**

✱ Follow all the instructions carefully to make sure you use all the equipment and materials in a safe way.

✱ Stand back from anything that's moving fast, or that involves eruptions or explosions. And don't throw, shoot, or whirl things around unless you're completely sure there's no one nearby.

And remember...

Always do experiments somewhere that's easy to clean up, like a kitchen or bathroom—NOT on the fancy carpet! And make sure you do clean up after yourself. Some of these experiments are messy!

So, are you ready to see some science?
Step this way ...

NOISY EXPERIMENTS

These experiments make loud bangs, weird noises, or cool music, to help you find out what sound really is, and how it works.

What is sound?
Basically, we hear sound when things move and vibrate, or shake quickly to and fro. These movements make the air vibrate, too. The vibrations spread out through the air and reach our ears.

Sound waves
When you drop an object into liquid it makes the water move, and ripples spread out in a circle until they touch the edge. Sound is the same, but instead of spreading out in a flat layer, the sound waves go in all directions.

Moving & shaking

For example, if someone hits a cymbal, the metal vibrates, and that makes invisible ripples, or sound waves, spread out in the air all around it. You hear the sound when the sound waves reach your ears.

Make a noise!

There are lots of ways to make a sound by getting something to vibrate. Try this simple experiment with a balloon:

1. Blow up a balloon, but don't tie it closed.

2. Hold the sides of the opening of the balloon, and pull them away from each other.

3. Slowly let the air out of the balloon. Try stretching the opening tightly and less tightly as the air escapes to see if you can change the sound.

Watch it

Sound vibrations are often so small or so fast that they can be hard to see clearly. But in this case, you should be able to see the neck of the balloon vibrating in a blur.

HOW DOES IT WORK?

As the air pushes through the narrow gap in the opening, it makes the rubbery balloon skin vibrate. This makes a loud squeaking sound.

GLITTER DISCO

This experiment will let you see the vibrations that sounds make—and get some glitter to dance!

WHAT YOU'LL NEED:

* A large radio with a speaker on the front, or a hi-fi speaker
* Glitter flakes (not the powdery kind—larger flakes work better)
* A large plastic plate or round tray
* Plastic wrap (sometimes called clingfilm)

1. Tear off a large piece of plastic wrap and stretch it over the plate so that it's as flat and smooth as possible. Tuck the plastic wrap under the plate to hold it in place.

2. Get your radio or speaker, and lie it down so that the speaker part is facing upward. You may have to ask someone to hold it steady.

3. Put your plastic wrap-covered plate right over the middle of the speaker. If you can see two speaker openings, use the bigger one if there is one.

4. Shake a small amount of glitter onto the middle of the plastic wrap—about a teaspoonful. (Be careful not to spill glitter into the speaker.)

HOW DOES IT WORK?
When the speaker makes sound, the sound makes vibrations in the air. They pass through the plate into the plastic wrap, making it vibrate up and down. Louder sounds make bigger vibrations! This makes the glitter jump in the air and move in time to the music.

5. Play some music—something with a clear beat, like rock, disco, or dance music—and turn it up loud (or as loud as you're allowed!).

Want to try making something else dance—or don't have any glitter? Lots of other things work well. Try small sequins, flaky sea salt, or small seeds, like caraway or sesame seeds.

STRAW TROMBONE

If you have a real trombone and know how to play it, you'll definitely be able to make a racket. But if not, here's the next best thing—a working trombone made out of household items!

WHAT YOU'LL NEED:

* Two straws, one slightly wider than the other
* A piece of thin cardboard at least 6 x 6 inches (15 x 15cm)
* A pencil
* Scissors
* Clear tape

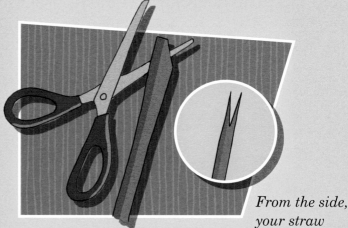

From the side, your straw should look like this.

1. Take the narrower straw, and flatten one end of it between your fingers. Then use the scissors to carefully snip off the sides to form a point.

2. Press the end again until it's as flat as you can make it. Then test it to see if it makes a sound. Put the cut end of the straw about 1 inch (3cm) inside in your mouth, and blow hard. If there's no sound, press the end flat again.

3. Copy this shape onto the cardboard, making it about 6 inches (15cm) across, and cut it out. Curve it into a cone, with a straw-sized hole at the top, and tape in place. Stick one end of the wider straw into the cone, and tape together.

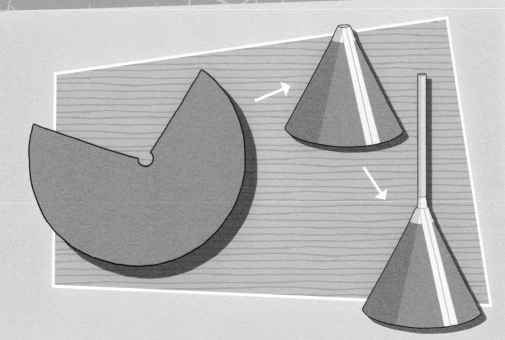

4. Now slide the wider straw over the narrower straw, so that it can slide up and down. Your trombone is ready to play!

HOW DOES IT WORK?

When you blow into the straw, your breath makes the pieces at the cut end vibrate, and this makes a noise. The air inside the straws vibrates, too. The longer the tube, the more space the air has to vibrate, and lower the sound will be. The cone, or "bell," on the end of the trombone helps to make the sound louder.

Can you use the sliding movement to make higher and lower notes? This will work best if the straws are only slightly different sizes and fit together tightly.

11

SCI-FI SOUNDS

With nothing more than a metal spring toy and a paper cup, you can make a sound like a sci-fi spaceship zapping an alien enemy with a laser gun. Try it and see!

WHAT YOU'LL NEED:

* A metal spring toy, the type that "walks" down stairs
* A paper cup
* Clear tape
* Pointy scissors or a craft knife
* A metal spoon or fork

⚠ ASK AN ADULT!

1. Ask an adult to cut two small, horizontal slots near the bottom of the cup, using the scissors or knife. They should be right next to the base of the cup, just above it.

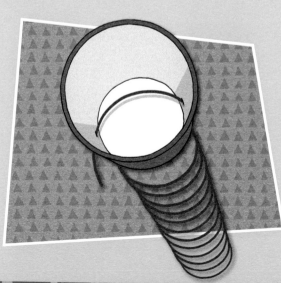

2. Now take the end of the spring toy and carefully slide it through both the slots, so that the first part of the spring lies flat against the cup base.

3. Hold the cup up in the air, so that the spring toy dangles down, almost touching the floor. (You might need to stand on a chair for this.)

HOW DOES IT WORK?
The space-age sound is created by lots of vibrations moving up the spring from the ground. The faster vibrations make higher-pitched sounds, which reach the cup first, followed by the lower ones. This makes the metallic "Pneeeeow!" noise that sounds like a space weapon.

To make the sound louder, tape a piece of cardboard around the cup in a cone shape to act as a megaphone.

4. To make the ray gun effect, make the spring toy bounce off the floor. The sound will come out of the cup. You can also try hitting the spring with the spoon.

BOTTLE BAGPIPE

This bizarre instrument makes a noise a bit like a bagpipe—or maybe a buzzing fly, or a ship's foghorn. See what you think it sounds like!

WHAT YOU'LL NEED:

* A small or medium-sized drinks bottle made of tough plastic
* A balloon
* Pointy scissors
* A straw
* Clear tape
* Paper

(!) ASK AN ADULT!

1.

Ask an adult to cut the top off the bottle as neatly as possible. Then ask them to make a small hole in the side of the bottle, the same size as the straw, by sticking the pointy tip of the scissors into the plastic and twisting it around.

2.

Next, cut the open end off the balloon and stretch it as tightly as you can over the open end of the bottle. When it's as tight and flat as you can get it, fix the edge to the bottle with sticky tape.

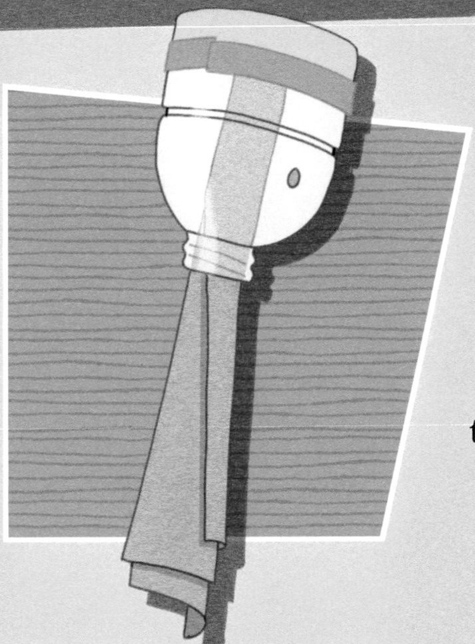

3.

Roll a piece of paper into a tight tube and stick it through the neck of the bottle, so that it presses against the balloon. Let it go so that it unrolls itself slightly and fits tightly into the bottle neck.

4.

Now stick the straw through the hole in the bottle.

5.

Hold the bottle in one hand and the paper tube in the other. Pushing the paper tube gently against the balloon, blow hard into the straw.

HOW DOES IT WORK?

When you blow air into the bottle, it pushes against the balloon and makes it vibrate. The vibrations spread into the paper tube, too, making a noise that comes out of the end of the tube.

SMARTPHONE SPEAKERS

These fantastic speakers will turn the tinny sound of a smartphone into a homemade boombox. All you need are some paper cups and a kitchen roll tube.

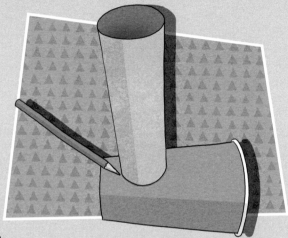

WHAT YOU'LL NEED:
- ★ The tube from the inside of a kitchen roll
- ★ 2 paper cups
- ★ A pencil
- ★ Pointy scissors
- ★ A smartphone with music stored on it

⚠ **ASK AN ADULT!**

1. Hold the end of the tube against the side of one of the cups, close to the bottom. Draw around the tube with the pencil to make a circle.

> If you don't have a kitchen roll tube, you can use part of a poster tube, or the cardboard tube from inside a roll of wrapping paper. Ask an adult to cut it to about 10 inches (25cm) long.

2. Cut out the circle, with an adult's help, cutting very slightly inside the line you have drawn. Then do the same thing with the other cup.

3. Hold the end of your smartphone against the middle of the tube, and draw around it with the pencil. Ask an adult to help you cut out the shape, cutting just inside the line.

4. Now push the ends of the tube into the holes in the paper cups, as far as they will go.

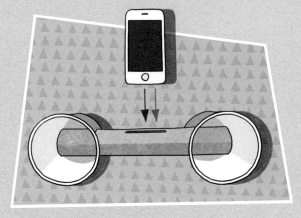

5. Stand the speakers on a table. Start some music playing on the phone, and push it into the hole in the tube.

HOW DOES IT WORK?

When the smartphone plays music, the vibrations spread out in all directions, so they don't sound very loud. When the phone is in the speakers, the vibrations spread into the tube, and then into the paper cups and the air inside them. This collects the sound and makes it point in one direction, so it sounds louder.

WHIRLING WHIRRER

Whirl this around your head and it will make a weird whirring sound. The secret is in the rubber band—make sure you use a really wide one!

WHAT YOU'LL NEED:

* ✸ A 6-inch (15-cm) ruler
* ✸ A short but thick rubber band, about ½ inch (1cm) wide
* ✸ A piece of string about 3 feet (1m) long
* ✸ A postcard
* ✸ Craft foam
* ✸ Scissors
* ✸ Clear tape

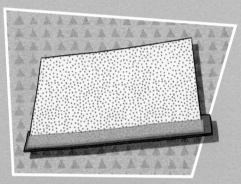

1. First, tape one edge of the postcard to the ruler, so that it sticks out slightly to one side, like this.

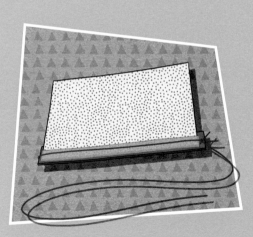

2. Tie one end of the string lengthwise around the ruler, and tape it in place too.

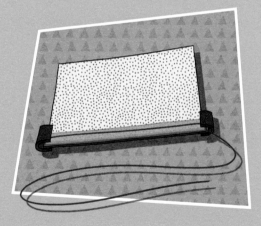

3. Cut two pieces of craft foam, each about ½ x 2 inches (1.5 x 5cm). Fold them around the ends of the ruler, letting the long end of the string hang free.

What could possibly go wrong? You could whack someone on the head or knock everything off a shelf, that's what! So make sure you ONLY do this in a large room with no one else in the way.

4. Stretch the rubber band around the ruler and over the pieces of foam.

5. Now hold the other end of the string, find a nice big empty space, and whirl the whirrer fast around your head.

HOW DOES IT WORK?

As the whirrer flies around, the air pushes against the rubber band and makes it vibrate, making a noise. When the whirrer moves faster, the rubber band vibrates faster, which makes a higher-pitched sound. The postcard helps to keep the whirrer flat as it flies. The air rushing past it pushes the postcard from above and below, making the whirrer stay level.

WHY DO BALLOONS POP?

Balloons are fun, but sooner or later they POP! What makes that loud popping noise, and why? Banish nervous people to a different room for this loud experiment!

WHAT YOU'LL NEED:
* ✷ Several balloons
* ✷ A candle and candle holder
* ✷ Matches
* ✷ Paper
* ✷ Scissors
* ✷ A pin for popping!

⊙ ASK AN ADULT!

1.
Blow up your balloons and tie them closed. Keep them in a safe place away from your experiment area.

2.
Cut some little figures out of your paper, with rectangles at the bottom, like this. Fold the rectangles flat so your figures will stand up.

3.

Hold a balloon about 6 inches (15cm) away from your paper figures, and pop the balloon with a pin. What happens to the people?

4.

Ask an adult to put your candle in its holder and light it with a match. Again, hold a balloon 6 inches (15cm) away and pop it with a pin. What happens to the candle?

HOW DOES IT WORK?

When you blow up a balloon, you fill it with lots of air. The air is under a lot of pressure—it's tightly squashed inside the balloon. When you pop a balloon, the squashed air suddenly escapes. It rushes outward at high speed. This makes a strong ripple in the air, called a pressure wave. It hits your ears as a loud bang and can also blow out a candle or blow over a paper figure.

Explosions cause a pressure wave too. That's why when there's an explosion, the things around it can get blown apart or blown away.

HOW FAST IS SOUND?

By now you know that when something makes a sound, sound waves travel through the air from where the sound started to your ears. In this experiment, you can see how long this takes.

WHAT YOU'LL NEED:

* ★ At least two people
* ★ A really big wide open space, like a playing field, sandy beach, or large playground
* ★ 2 pan lids

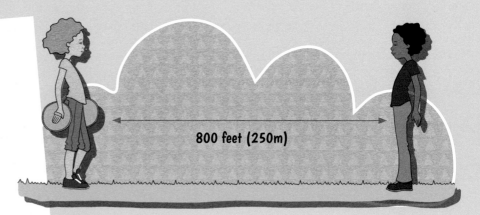

800 feet (250m)

1. One person should take both the pan lids and move really far away from the other person—ideally 800 feet (250m) away or more. But they should still be able to see each other.

2. The first person should bang the pan lids together once, loudly. When the second person *sees* the lids bang together, they should stick one hand in the air.

Bang!

HOW DOES IT WORK?

When the first person bangs the pan lids, the other person sees it pretty much straight away because the speed of light is so incredibly fast. However, the speed of sound is much slower. This means that the sound of the bang takes a while to catch up as the sound spreads out through the air.

3. Then, when the second person *hears* the sound of the lids banging together, they should stick their other hand up.

4.

If you have someone else to help too, they could use a timer or stopwatch to try to measure the difference between seeing and hearing the bang.

If you want, try some math, too. Measure the distance between the two people and the time the sound takes to travel. With these (and maybe an adult to help), can you work out a figure for the speed of sound? It may be easier to calculate the figure using metric measurements, so it might look something like this:

Distance: 300m
Sound travel time: about 1 second
Speed: 300m per second
Speed in km per hour: ?
SPEED IN MILES PER HOUR: ?

MESSY EXPERIMENTS

As every scientist knows, some experiments are messier than others. The experiments in this chapter involve gloopy slime, paint splats, messy explosions, or just getting soaking wet. Get your old clothes on!

MESSY SCIENCE
So what type of experiments make the most mess, and why?

Chemical reactions
A chemical reaction happens when two different chemicals or substances mix together and react, or change. Not all chemicals react together, but when they do, it can certainly be messy.

Messy materials
Experimenting with water, oil, eggs, paint, or other messy stuff is never going to be neat and tidy.

Explosions
Not forgetting, of course, crazy explosions that shoot everything in all directions. There are many ways to create an explosion, and you'll find a few in the following pages.

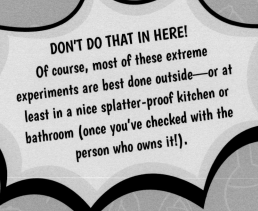

Make a mini mess

For starters, try this simple experiment to see a basic chemical reaction at work. (Hold on to the ingredients, as you'll be needing them again soon.)

You'll need white vinegar and baking soda—both available in a supermarket.

Put a small cup or glass in a bowl, and add some vinegar to the cup or glass until it's about half full. Then get a heaped teaspoon of baking soda, and drop it in the vinegar. What happens?

HOW DOES IT WORK?

In a chemical reaction, chemicals combine and change to make new chemicals. In this experiment, the vinegar and the baking soda react to make a gas called carbon dioxide. The gas makes lots of bubbles that make the mixture foam up. The reaction also makes other chemicals. Luckily for you, they're harmless! But some reactions aren't so safe. Sometimes they can create dangerous chemicals, explosions, or flames. So always follow the instructions carefully, and don't mix the wrong things together!

THE EXPLODING BAG

This experiment reveals the true power of a chemical reaction taking place inside a plastic bag. Stand well back!

WHAT YOU'LL NEED:

* White vinegar
* Baking soda (sometimes known as bicarbonate of soda)
* Warm water
* A tablespoon
* A measuring cup or average-sized drinking cup
* A plastic food or freezer bag
* A piece of kitchen roll or tissue
* A big outdoor space

Some food bags have a seal that you can press tightly closed. If you don't have this type, use a large sandwich bag that you can tie a tight knot in instead.

1. Lay the piece of kitchen paper or tissue flat and put 2 tablespoons of baking soda into the middle.

2. Fold the paper up so that the powder is held safely inside, like this.

3. Put about a quarter of a cup of warm water from a hot faucet into the bag. Then add about half a cup of vinegar. Hold the bag upright so that the liquid doesn't spill out.

This is easier with two people—one to hold the paper up, the other to close the bag.

4. Go outside, if you aren't there already. Now put the folded-up paper inside the bag, but keep it away from the liquid. Seal or tie up the bag tightly so no air can escape.

HOW DOES IT WORK?

The vinegar and baking soda react and make carbon dioxide gas (the warm water helps to speed things up). As more and more gas is made, it fills up the bag and tries to escape. Finally, the bag can't hold it in any more, and ... SPLAT!

5. Once the bag is sealed shut, let the paper parcel drop into the liquid. Put the bag down on the ground and wait to see what happens!

To make an even messier splat, use runny water-based paint instead of water!

FIZZ FOUNTAIN

This famous experiment makes messy foaming cola splurt all over the place. Some versions of this experiment use candy, but salt works even better!

WHAT YOU'LL NEED:
* A big bottle of diet cola
* A bag of salt
* A piece of paper
* An outdoor space

Don't keep the cola in the fridge—it works better if it's at room temperature.

1. Open the cola and stand it in a safe place, outdoors and away from anything that you don't want to get messy.

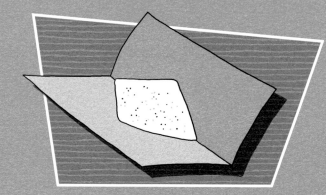

2. Fold your piece of paper in half and pour salt into the fold. Use as much salt as you can comfortably hold in the paper.

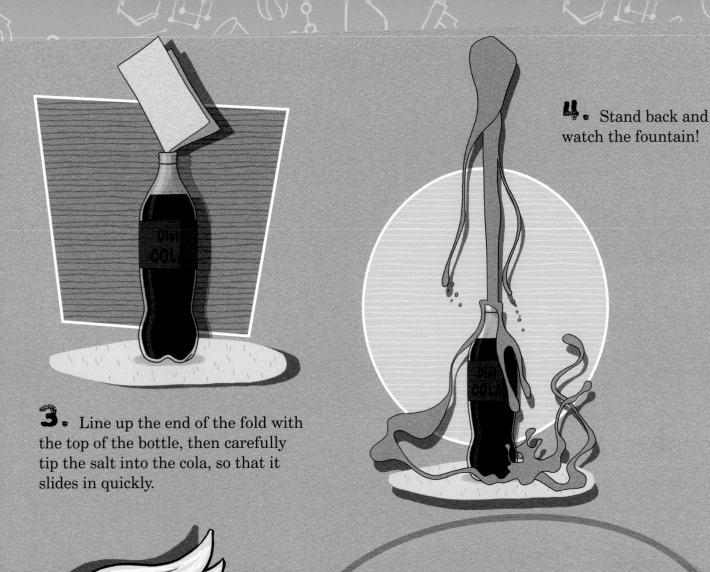

4. Stand back and watch the fountain!

3. Line up the end of the fold with the top of the bottle, then carefully tip the salt into the cola, so that it slides in quickly.

HOW DOES IT WORK?

Fizzy drinks contain a lot of carbon dioxide gas, which is dissolved in the liquid. Normally, the bubbles of gas come out of the drink gradually. But the salt makes it come out much faster. Scientists think this is because the rough surfaces of the salt granules give the gas something to stick to, and it forms large bubbles. Suddenly, there's so much gas that it can't fit in the bottle, so the foamy cola shoots out.

Don't worry about having cola and salt in the same meal. An explosion only happens when a lot of salt and cola are mixed together very quickly (cola with chips might make you burp, though).

29

HOMEMADE LAVA LAMP

A lava lamp makes bubbles of colorful hot wax float up and down inside a glass bottle. You can make your own simple version with oil, water, and food coloring.

WHAT YOU'LL NEED:

- ✸ A tall, clear container, such as a glass jar or bottle
- ✸ A bottle of sunflower oil (the type used for cooking)
- ✸ Warm water
- ✸ Liquid food coloring
- ✸ Baking powder
- ✸ A spoon

If you don't have baking powder, you could use a fizzing bath bomb broken into small pieces, or a fizzy anti-indigestion drink tablet.

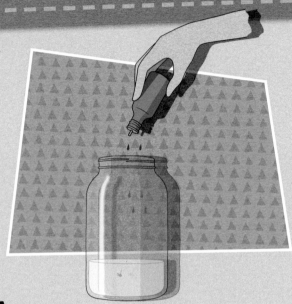

1. First, pour some warm water from the hot faucet into your glass container, until it's about a quarter full. Add a few drops of food coloring in your favorite color.

2. Carefully pour in sunflower oil until the container is about three-quarters full. The liquids will swirl about so give them a few moments to settle.

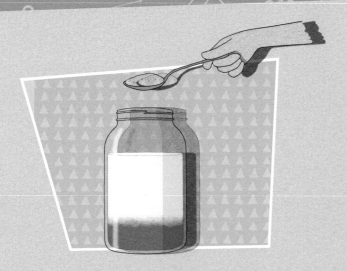

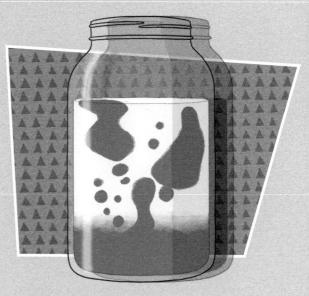

3. Now take a spoonful of baking powder and drop it into the container. If it sits on top of the oil at first, push it down with the spoon.

4. Watch the container from the side to see what happens.

HOW DOES IT WORK?

The baking powder contains chemicals that react with the water to make gas bubbles. The water is heavier than the oil, so the oil floats on top of it. But the bubbles are lighter, so they float to get to the top of the oil. They slowly force their way up through the oil, taking some of the colored water with them.

GRAVITY SPLATS

Use gravity to make paint splat and you can get all kinds of interesting results. It's art and science—all rolled up into one simple experiment!

WHAT YOU'LL NEED:

★ Large pieces of paper, or a roll of drawing paper or plain wallpaper

★ Water-based poster paint or powder paint in different colors

★ Water

★ Lots of plastic or paper bowls

★ Rubber balls or pebbles

★ Large spoons

★ Old clothes and newspapers

⚠ ASK AN ADULT!

1. First, lay down newspapers to catch any mess. Then make runny paint by mixing the paint or paint powder with water in the bowls. Put a bowl of paint on the paper, then drop a rubber ball or pebble into it. Splat!

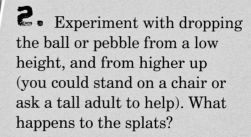

You don't have to use paper—if you have a patio, sidewalk, or playground to use, you can splat straight onto that! But make sure you get permission first.

2. Experiment with dropping the ball or pebble from a low height, and from higher up (you could stand on a chair or ask a tall adult to help). What happens to the splats?

3. For another splat method, simply get a spoonful of paint, lift it up, and tip it out onto the paper or the ground. Again, try dropping it from lower and higher up.

If you used paper, you could let it dry, then put your splat artwork on the wall.

4. If you like, try measuring the height you drop from, and comparing this to the size of the splat you make.

HOW DOES IT WORK?

Objects that are dropped from higher up make a bigger splat. Maybe that's what you expected. But why does it happen? When objects fall, they start off completely still, then speed up. The farther they fall, the faster they go. A faster object hits the ground or the paper much harder, and this forces the paint to splat out farther.

STREAM OF LIGHT

Light always travels in straight lines ... or does it? In this experiment you can make a beam of light travel along a curved stream of water.

WHAT YOU'LL NEED:
* ✹ A large, clear, plastic drinks bottle
* ✹ Sharp, pointy scissors
* ✹ Water
* ✹ A large bucket, sink, or bathtub to catch the water
* ✹ A bright flashlight or laser pointer

! ASK AN ADULT!

1. Ask an adult to make a small hole, about ¼ inch (0.5cm) across, near the bottom of the bottle. They can do this by carefully sticking the pointed tip of the scissors in and twisting it around.

2. Cover the hole with a finger, and fill the bottle to the brim with water. Stand the bottle on a flat surface next to the bucket, sink, or bathtub, with the hole facing it.

Get a friend to help you with this step.

3. Turn off the lights in the room so that you can see the flashlight light better. Switch on the flashlight or laser pointer and shine it from behind the bottle, through the water inside, and toward the hole.

4. Remove the finger and let the water flow out. You should see light flowing along the stream of water. Put your hand under it to see if it makes a spot of light on your skin.

HOW DOES IT WORK?

Light does travel in straight lines, but it also bounces, or reflects, off shiny surfaces. When light enters the water stream, it reflects off the inside surface of the water. It bounces to and fro inside the water stream, following its path.

This is the science behind fiber-optic technology, which carries light along tiny glass tubes. As light moves so fast, fiber optic cables can be used to carry lots of information in the form of light signals. They're often used as internet cables.

SLO-MO WATER BALL

What would happen if you popped a balloon full of water on the International Space Station? This experiment might give you some idea!

WHAT YOU'LL NEED:

* ✹ A balloon
* ✹ Water
* ✹ String
* ✹ Something to hang the balloon from, such as a low tree-branch or washing line
* ✹ A pin
* ✹ A smartphone or digital camera with a slow-motion filming option

1. Blow the balloon up to stretch it, then let it go down. To fill it with water, stretch the neck of the balloon over a faucet, and run the faucet slowly. You only need to fill the balloon to about half the usual size.

2. Tie the balloon closed, and tie some string around the knot. Hang the balloon up somewhere outdoors, away from anything you don't want to get wet!

3. Ask a friend to film the balloon on a slow-motion setting while you pop it (or you could set up the camera to do this by itself, using a tripod). Don't let your phone or camera get wet.

4. Once the camera is running, take the pin and gently pop the balloon. You need to do it gently so that the balloon stays as still as possible. Then play back what happened!

HOW DOES IT WORK?

Thanks to Earth's gravity, when you pop the balloon the water will soon splat all over the ground. But when you view it in slow motion, you'll see that the popped balloon shrinks away very fast, before the water has a chance to start falling. For a moment, a perfect balloon-shaped ball of water hangs in mid-air.

Astronauts have actually popped balloons full of water on the International Space Station. You could ask an adult to help you find a video of this on the Internet.

EGG-DROP CHALLENGE

In this "eggstreme" experiment, you have to come up with the best way to prevent a terrible mess. Can you work out how to give an egg a safe landing?

WHAT YOU'LL NEED:

* ✸ A box of eggs (not expensive ones!)
* ✸ A chair to stand on
* ✸ An outdoor space
* ✸ A selection of materials, such as straws, clear tape, cotton wool, cardboard, plastic bags, balloons, string, rubber bands

⚠ ASK AN ADULT!

1. Ask an adult to boil some eggs.

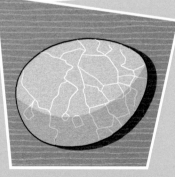

2. Now, stand on the chair and drop an egg onto the ground from as high in the air as you can. Crack! The egg breaks because the force of it hitting the ground cracks its shell.

3. Your challenge is to build a wrapper, holder, or protective suit for an egg that will allow it to fall to the ground without breaking. Use the materials to try to cushion the egg or break its fall. Wrapping your egg in cotton balls might work.

4. Or perhaps you could make a protective cage for your egg using straws. If you have several people, you can all take an egg each and have a competition to see who can make the best egg protector.

If you're stuck for ideas, how about...
- A plastic-bag parachute to slow down the egg's fall
- A cushioned "airbag" made from inflated balloons or sandwich bags
- A bouncy egg hammock made from rubber bands

5. When the inventions are ready, each person can test their creation by standing on the chair and dropping their egg. Did any of the eggs survive the fall?

HOW DOES IT WORK?
Eggs have strong shells that can withstand some pressure, such as the weight of a mother hen sitting on them. However, a sudden impact will break the shell. The best way to keep the egg safe is to slow down its impact with the ground.

CONFETTI CANNON

This simple shooter made from a balloon and a cup will fire a huge burst of confetti into the air. Perfect for parties! (As long as you don't mind a massive mess, that is ...)

WHAT YOU'LL NEED:

* ★ A paper cup
* ★ A balloon
* ★ Scissors or a craft knife
* ★ Clear tape
* ★ Confetti

⚠ ASK AN ADULT!

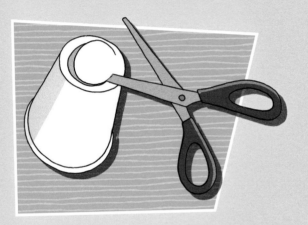

1. Ask an adult to cut out the bottom of the paper cup using a craft knife or sharp scissors.

You can buy confetti at craft and stationery stores—or make your own by cutting colored paper or tissue paper into little pieces. You can also use a hole punch to make lots of holes in colored paper, then collect all the tiny circles that fall out.

2. Cut the round end off a balloon, and tie a knot in the neck end. Then stretch it over the bottom of your paper cup, and sticky tape it firmly in place.

3. Now pour your confetti into the cup— and keep it somewhere safe until the moment comes to fire it!

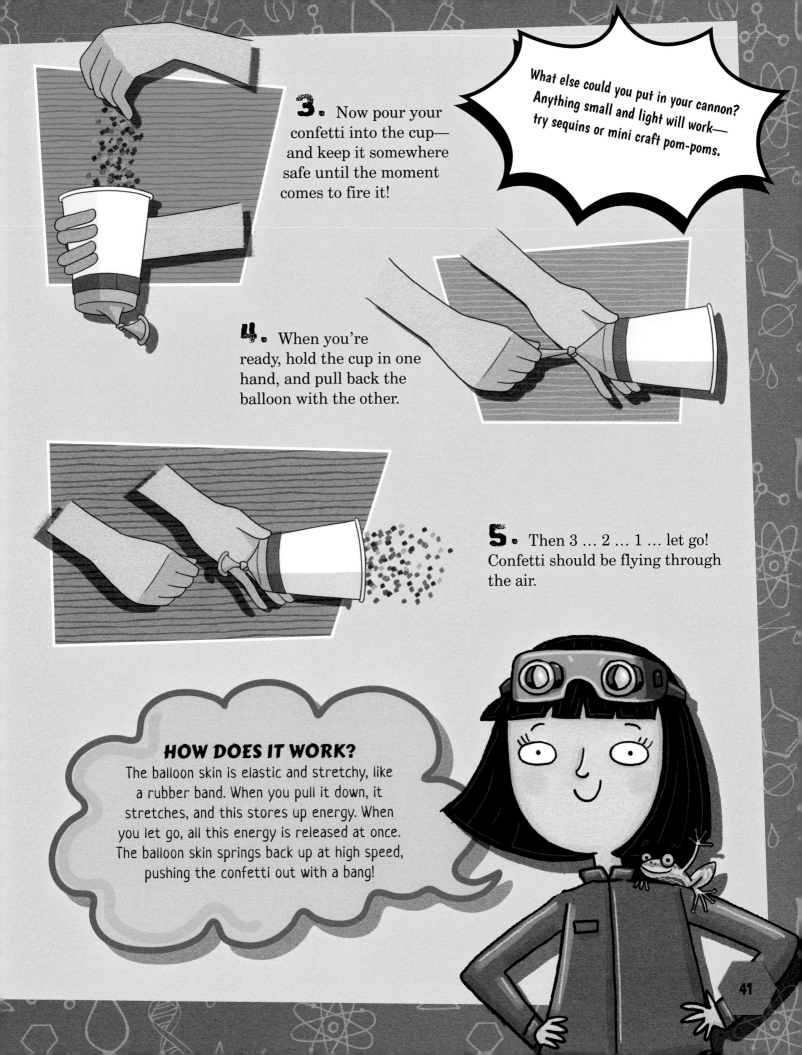

What else could you put in your cannon? Anything small and light will work— try sequins or mini craft pom-poms.

4. When you're ready, hold the cup in one hand, and pull back the balloon with the other.

5. Then 3 ... 2 ... 1 ... let go! Confetti should be flying through the air.

HOW DOES IT WORK?

The balloon skin is elastic and stretchy, like a rubber band. When you pull it down, it stretches, and this stores up energy. When you let go, all this energy is released at once. The balloon skin springs back up at high speed, pushing the confetti out with a bang!

ODD OOBLECK

This strange substance is named after the green slime in a book by the famous writer, Dr. Seuss. It's easy to make, but behaves in some very odd ways ...

WHAT YOU'LL NEED:

* ✱ One or more packets of cornstarch
* ✱ Water
* ✱ A measuring pitcher
* ✱ A large, shallow, plastic food container or mixing bowl
* ✱ Green food coloring (optional)
* ✱ Old clothes and newspaper

1. Carefully pour your cornstarch into the measuring jug to check how much you have. Then tip the cornstarch into the container.

Oobleck is nontoxic, but messy—REALLY messy. Do this experiment in a kitchen or bathroom, and spread out newspapers to protect the surroundings. Or you could do it outdoors.

2. Measure out half as much water as you have cornstarch. For example, if you have 2 cups (600ml) of cornstarch, measure 1 cup (300ml) of water. Add a few drops of food coloring if you like.

3. Add some of the water to the cornstarch and mix it with your hands (this can take a while). Add more water, bit by bit, until you have a gloopy, slimy mixture.

4. Now try these tests to see what the mixture does.

- Grab a handful of oobleck and squeeze it tight. Then let go and open your hands out.
- Pour out a puddle of oobleck, then try to push your fingers through it quickly.

- Let a plastic toy figure sink into the oobleck as if it was quicksand, then try to pull it out quickly.

- Press your hand slowly into the oobleck—then try hitting it hard. What happens?

HOW DOES IT WORK?

Oobleck can behave like a solid or a liquid. When it's pressed hard, the ingredients lock together and it acts like a solid. But when it's handled gently, it flows like a liquid. In bigger and even messier experiments, people have filled swimming pools with oobleck and managed to run over the surface!

SPEEDY EXPERIMENTS

These experiments are all about making things move, which is an important part of science and technology. Understanding movement means we can make all kinds of vehicles, so that we can travel to school, the stores ... or even into space!

HOW MOVEMENT WORKS

To make things go, something needs to pull them or push against them. In other words, you need a force. There are lots of types of forces you can use, and you'll meet several of them in this chapter.

ROCKET POWER: When gas rushes out of something, it pushes that thing the other way.

PADDLE POWER: A moving paddle pushes against water, making a boat move.

ELASTIC POWER: Energy stored in something springy or elastic can be turned into movement.

GRAVITY: This pulling force makes things fall downward or roll downhill.

ELECTRICITY: An electrical spark is a flow of high-speed particles.

The ball test

To start with, try this movement experiment in a safe open space outdoors. You'll need two balls—a large one, like a basketball, and a smaller one, like a tennis ball or a bouncy rubber ball.

Hold the balls up with the smaller ball sitting right on top of the larger one, then drop them together. What happens?

If it works, you'll see the big ball bounce back up a little way, and the small ball zoom up really high!

HOW DOES IT WORK?

Movement is a kind of energy. If you put more energy in, you'll get more movement out. When the big ball drops, it hits the ground and bounces back up. Straight away it hits the small ball on top of it. Some of the movement energy from the big ball passes into the small ball. The small ball is lighter, so the extra energy makes it move much faster.

WATCH OUT!
Be careful when performing these high-speed experiments. Make sure you have plenty of space to work in, and stand well back from fast-moving objects.

45

BALLOON-POWERED CAR

Use the air shooting out of a balloon to drive a toy car forward. How fast can you make it go?

WHAT YOU'LL NEED:

* ✹ Strong, stiff cardboard
* ✹ Three straws
* ✹ Two wooden skewers
* ✹ Strong scissors
* ✹ Clear tape
* ✹ A marker pen
* ✹ A sharp pencil
* ✹ A balloon

⚠ ASK AN ADULT!

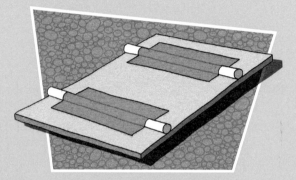

1. Cut a rectangle of cardboard the size of a small book. Cut two straws so they're the same width as (or just slightly longer than) the cardboard. Tape them to the cardboard.

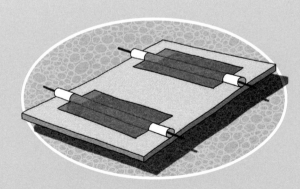

2. Ask an adult to use strong scissors to cut the wooden skewers so they are about 1 inch (2cm) longer than the cut straws. Thread the skewers through the straws.

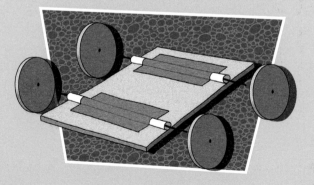

3. Draw around a round object onto some more cardboard to make four wheels, 3 inches (6cm) across. Cut them out and ask an adult to make a small hole in the middle of each one, using the pencil. Push the wheels onto the ends of the skewers, and turn your car over.

4. Blow the balloon up to stretch it, then let it down again. Now cut off the thick part at the opening, and stick your third straw inside. Wrap the tape around them both to make a tight seal.

5. Tape part of the straw onto the top of your car, with the open end overlapping the end of the cardboard. The balloon should rest on top of the car. Blow into the straw to inflate the balloon, then put the car on the ground and let it go!

HOW DOES IT WORK?

Blowing up the balloon fills it with squeezed, pressurized air. When you let it go, the air shoots out of the straw. The moving air pushes back on the straw, and this pushes the car along.

FLYING MARBLES

If you wanted to jump over a big gap, you'd take a big run-up. Help these marbles do the same with a high-speed jump ramp.

WHAT YOU'LL NEED:

* Marbles
* A foam pipe insulation tube, from a hardware store
* Scissors
* Heavy-duty packing tape or duct tape
* Books
* Removable clear tape
* A plastic bowl or container

(!) ASK AN ADULT!

If you have more tubes, you could make a really long channel. See if it's long enough to build a rollercoaster with a loop-the-loop.

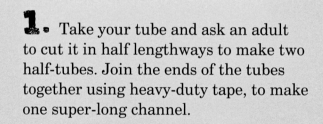

1. Take your tube and ask an adult to cut it in half lengthways to make two half-tubes. Join the ends of the tubes together using heavy-duty tape, to make one super-long channel.

2. Use removable clear tape to fix one end of the ramp to a door frame, and curve the lower end upward to make a ramp. Use a pile of books to support the ramp.

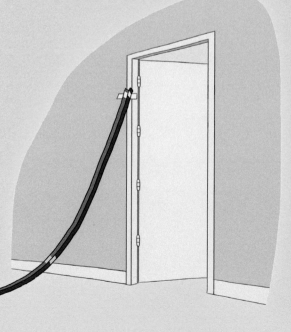

3. Hold a marble a little way up the slope, and let it go so that it rolls down. Try rolling the marble from higher up the slope, then try rolling it from the very top. What happens?

If you have them, experiment with different sizes of marble. Do bigger, heavier marbles roll faster or slower?

4. Put the plastic bowl near the end of the ramp, and try to roll marbles from the top so that they fly off the ramp and land in the bowl. It's not as easy as it looks!

HOW DOES IT WORK?

As a ball rolls down a slope, it starts off slowly. But as gravity keeps pulling on it, it picks up speed and goes faster and faster, or "accelerates." The higher up it starts, the faster it will go. Marbles that have picked up a lot of speed will fly off the end of the ramp and jump a big gap.

AIR-POWERED ROCKET

Fancy flying your very own spacecraft? Follow these steps to build your own rocket ship, which uses air pressure to shoot high in the air.

WHAT YOU'LL NEED:

* An empty, clean, plastic detergent or drinks bottle
* A straw
* Modeling clay or poster putty
* Paper
* Marker pens
* Scissors
* Clear tape

1. First, make your rocket. Cut a rectangle of paper about 2 x 3 inches (5 x 8cm), and roll it around the straw. Tape it in place to make a tube. It should be a snug fit, but not too tight. The paper should be able to slide up and down the straw easily.

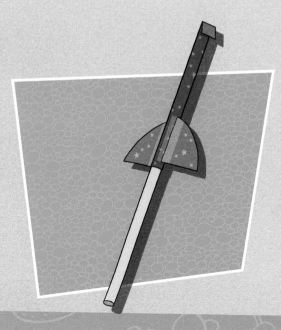

2. Fold over and flatten the end of the paper to make your rocket's nose. You can also add paper fins to its base to help it fly.

You could use more paper to draw a large, round moon to act as a target for your rocket. See if you can hit it right in the middle.

3. Roll a ball of modeling clay or poster putty slightly bigger than the neck of the bottle. Wrap it around the straw so that the end sticks out, making sure the straw is not squashed flat. Fit the ball and the straw tightly onto the bottle neck, like this.

4. Now squeeze the bottle hard and watch your rocket fly. How high can you make it go?

HOW DOES IT WORK?

The bottle rocket launcher is full of air. When you squeeze it suddenly, air is forced down the straw and pushes hard against the rocket on the end, firing it forward at high speed.

51

ANTI-GRAVITY CUP

If you fill a cup with water and then turn it upside down, the water will fall out ... won't it? Not if it's flying fast enough!

WHAT YOU'LL NEED:

* ✸ A disposable paper or plastic cup
* ✸ Strong string
* ✸ Strong clear tape or duct tape
* ✸ Pointy scissors
* ✸ Water
* ✸ Nerves of steel

(!) ASK AN ADULT!

1. Ask an adult to make two holes in the cup, one on either side just below the rim, using the pointy scissors.

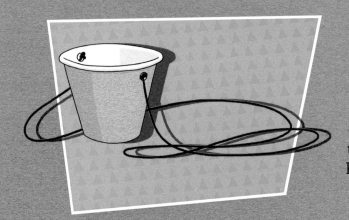

2. Cut a piece of string about 6 feet (2m) long, and thread the ends through the holes. Tie each end on firmly, so that the string makes a long handle.

3. Put tape over the holes to make the join stronger. Now pour water into the cup until it's about half full.

If you don't want to use water, or are doing this indoors, you could put beads, small candies, or small uncooked pasta shapes in the cup instead.

4. You'll need to do this bit outdoors. Holding the end of the loop of string, quickly swing the cup over and over in a complete circle. At certain points, the cup will be upside down, but no water should come out.

HOW DOES IT WORK?

If the cup whirls around fast enough, the water will not fall out, even when it's upside down. Sir Isaac Newton's Laws of Motion tell us that a moving object wants to continue in the same direction unless another force acts on it. You've supplied a force called centripetal force by pulling on the string. It's even stronger, pulling on the cup, than the force of gravity working on the water, so the base of the cup catches up with and holds the water.

MAKE TINY LIGHTNING!

We're not joking ... in this experiment you really can make a flash of lightning, just like the lightning you see in a thunderstorm. The only difference is it's really, really tiny! (And a lot safer ...)

WHAT YOU'LL NEED:
* A balloon
* A metal spoon
* A completely dark room

1. First, get your room ready. Unless it has no windows, it will be easiest to make it really dark when it's also dark outside. Switch off the lights, any screens, and machines with LEDs.

2. Outside the room (so you can see what you're doing), blow up the balloon and tie it. Hold the spoon in one hand and the balloon in the other. Now rub the balloon on your hair, quite fast, for a long time—at least a minute.

Yes, you'll get super-messy hair. Sorry about that!

3. Keeping the balloon and the spoon apart, and not touching anything, go into the dark room (getting someone else to close the door for you).

HOW DOES IT WORK?

The rubbing makes tiny things called electrons come off your hair and onto the balloon. These extra electrons build up and give the balloon an electric charge, called static electricity. When the spoon comes near the balloon, the electrons jump across the gap as a spark of electricity.

4. Now hold the balloon up in front of you, and slowly move the spoon toward it. If you've rubbed the balloon enough, a mini lightning spark will zap across the gap!

SURFACE SPEED

You can't see it, but the surface of water has a strange "skin" on it that can make it behave in weird ways. It's called surface tension.

WHAT YOU'LL NEED:
* A large, shallow bowl or plate
* A pitcher
* Water
* Glitter or black pepper
* Dishwashing liquid
* Craft foam
* Scissors

1. Put the bowl on a flat surface and carefully fill it with water, using the pitcher. When the surface is calm and flat, gently sprinkle some glitter or pepper onto it. It should mostly stay on the surface.

2. Squeeze a little washing-up liquid onto the tip of your finger. Then dip your finger into the water, right in the middle. What happens?

A tiny lizard, called a pygmy gecko, can use surface tension to walk on water.

3. Clean the plate or bowl and start again with fresh water. This time, cut a small surfboard shape out of the craft foam, like this. Make a little notch in the back. Put the surfboard in the water. It should float motionless on the surface.

As well as pepper or glitter, surface tension can hold up larger objects, such as metal pins and paper clips. Try it! Then try adding some dishwashing liquid to the water.

4. Now take the surfboard out of the water, and use your finger to put a blob of dishwashing liquid into the notch. Put the surfboard back in the water and watch it go!

HOW DOES IT WORK?

The molecules that make up water have a force that makes them pull toward each other. On the surface they pull more strongly, creating surface tension. This makes it hard for small objects to break the surface, so they stay on top. Dishwashing liquid breaks up the surface tension, causing the water molecules (and the pepper and surfboard) to be drawn toward the unaffected water. This makes the pepper and the surfboard move.

ELASTIC TUB BOAT

This isn't a tug boat, it's a tub boat! It has a rotating paddle to push it forward, just like some real boats. Make two and have a race!

WHAT YOU'LL NEED:

* A clean, dry, plastic ice cream tub or margarine tub, with a lid
* Two popsicle sticks
* Heavy-duty tape or duct tape
* A rubber band, slightly longer than the width of the tub
* Scissors
* ⚠ ASK AN ADULT!

Another way to stick them on is to use a hot glue gun, but you'll need to ask an adult to do this for you.

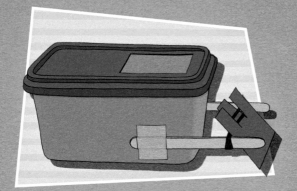

1. Use the tape to attach the sticks onto the tub, one on each side, just above the base. About half of each stick should stick out at one end, like this.

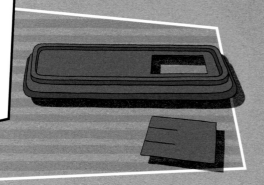

2. Now take the plastic lid, and ask an adult to cut a square out of it, about 2 x 2 inches (5 x 5cm). Cut two slots, 1 inch (2cm) apart, from one side of the square up to the middle.

3. Loop your rubber band around the ends of the two sticks. Then slot the plastic square onto one side of the rubber band, using the two cuts, to make a paddle.

4. Hold the boat and turn the paddle around and around so that it makes the rubber band twist. Keep going until the rubber band is tightly twisted.

5. Put the boat into calm water in a bathtub or paddling pool, and watch it go!

HOW DOES IT WORK?

As the rubber band gets twisted around and around, it gets stretched. This stores up a supply of energy. When you let the paddle go, the rubber band un-stretches, which makes it unwind, using that stored energy to turn the paddle. Each time the paddle turns, it pushes against the water, making the boat move along.

EXPLODING ROCKET

Use the explosive power of a baking soda and vinegar reaction to send a rocket up, up, and away.

WHAT YOU'LL NEED:

★ A small plastic tube-shaped container with a tight-fitting pop-off lid

★ Craft cardboard

★ Scissors

★ Clear tape

★ Felt-tip pens

★ Baking soda (sometimes known as bicarbonate of soda)

★ A teaspoon

★ White vinegar

★ A smooth, flat surface outdoors, with lots of space around it

(!) ASK AN ADULT!

An old-style photographic film canister makes a perfect rocket. Vitamin tablets and beads often come in this kind of container too.

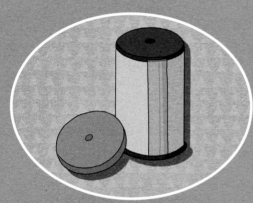

1. First, take the lid off your plastic tube, and roll a piece of cardboard around it to make a rocket shape. Tape it in place so that the open end of the tube is at the bottom.

2. Cut a circle of cardboard slightly wider than your rocket, then cut a slot in it from the side to the middle. Shape it into a nose cone for the rocket, and tape it on.

3. Cut cardboard triangles to make four rocket fins. Tape them onto the rocket at the base, to help it stand up. You can also draw on windows, numbers, or other details.

4. Turn the lid from the tube upside-down, and carefully tip a teaspoon of baking soda into the middle. Turn the rocket over and half-fill the tube with vinegar.

Everyone should stand well back to watch the rocket take off. DON'T get too close or lean over it!

5. Ask an adult to quickly put the lid onto the tube, tipping the baking soda inside as they do so. They should press it on firmly, stand the rocket on the ground, and move away quickly!

HOW DOES IT WORK?

The vinegar and baking soda react to make bubbles of carbon dioxide gas. As more and more gas gets made, it presses hard against the inside of the container. Finally—if it works!—it pushes the lid off with a bang, and this pushes the rocket upward into the air.

AIR BLASTER

You can use forces to make cars, boats, and rockets go—but this is a bit different. The air blaster simply shoots air! It's completely safe, so you can aim it at many different objects.

WHAT YOU'LL NEED:
* A large, plastic drinks bottle
* A plastic bag, such as a sandwich bag
* Scissors
* A marker pen
* Strong clear tape or duct tape
* A strong rubber band

! ASK AN ADULT!

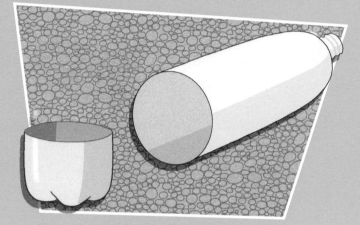

1. Ask an adult to cut the bottom end off the plastic bottle, as neatly as possible. Stand the bottle on the plastic bag, and draw a circle around it, about 1 inch (2cm) bigger than the bottle on all sides.

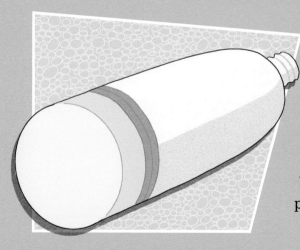

2. Carefully cut out the circle. Place the circle over the cut end of the bottle, and tape the edges to the bottle all the way around. Make the circle overlap the bottle by about ¼ inch (1cm), so that the plastic is slightly loose.

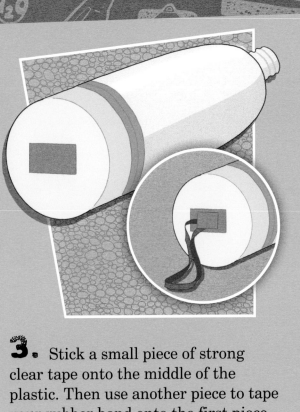

You can also use the air blaster to shoot at a target, such as a paper figure. Or ask an adult to light a candle, and see if you can use the blaster to blow it out from the other side of the room!

3. Stick a small piece of strong clear tape onto the middle of the plastic. Then use another piece to tape your rubber band onto the first piece to make a handle.

4. Now hold the bottle up and aim the open end at a target. Pull the rubber-band handle back, then let the handle go (keeping hold of the bottle while you do this). If you aimed right, a puff of air should hit your target—even if you're several yards away!

HOW DOES IT WORK?

When you pull the plastic back you suck extra air into the bottle. When you let the rubber band go, the air is suddenly pushed out. But it has to get through the narrower neck of the bottle, and to do this it has to speed up. This creates a spinning, doughnut-shaped movement of air called a vortex, which can travel a long way in one direction.

MYSTERIOUS EXPERIMENTS

Science can behave in some VERY strange ways. This section is full of experiments that make you go "Wow! How does that work!?" and "Wait—WHAT just happened!?" They're great for amazing your friends and family.

WHY IS SCIENCE SURPRISING?

Most of the time, our brains make good predictions about how objects and materials will behave, based on our past experiences. However, sometimes an experiment can make something behave in an unexpected way—it might even seem impossible! It's breaking the rules our brains have learned, but it's not breaking the rules of science. That's what will make you gasp!

Mysterious science

None of these things are magical—they all happen according to the rules of science. But the more you learn about science, the more you find out that it really IS quite bizarre. For instance, did you know that ...

A particle (tiny bit of matter) can actually be in two places at once.

Time can slow down if you're moving fast enough!

At very low temperatures, helium can flow against gravity.

Mobius madness

Let the weirdness begin with this fun mini experiment!

You need a strip of thin cardboard, about 1 inch (3cm) wide and 12 inches (30cm) long. Bring the ends together to make a loop, but before joining them together, flip one end over so that there's a twist in the strip. Then tape the ends together. The twisted strip is called a Mobius strip.

Take a pair of scissors with a pointy tip, and cut into the middle of the strip. Ask an adult to help if it's tricky.
Cut all the way along the middle until you get back to where you started.

You've cut the strip in half, right ...

HOW DOES IT WORK?

When you twist the end over, you join one edge of the strip to the other edge. Instead of two edges, it now has one long continuous edge. You can't cut it in two because one side is continuous with the other. Simple, isn't it?

... OR HAVE YOU???

AMAZIN' RAISIN

What do you mean, you've never dropped a raisin into your soda? You just have to try it! There's mysterious science at work.

WHAT YOU'LL NEED:

* A new bottle of colorless soda (such as Sprite® or 7 Up®)
* A tall, clear glass
* Raisins

This will work with most sodas, but clear ones make it easier for you to see what the raisins are up to.

1. Open the bottle and pour soda into the glass, filling it almost to the top. Wait for the bubbles to settle down (don't shake the bottle first!).

2. Take a few raisins (large ones works best) and gently drop them into the glass. Watch what they do. Give it a few minutes—it may take a little while to see what's happening.

3. If it works, your raisins will start to behave strangely. They'll sink to the bottom, wait there for a bit, then float up to the surface. After hanging around there for a while, they'll head back to the bottom—and repeat!

HOW DOES IT WORK?

The soda has carbon dioxide gas dissolved in it—this is what makes the bubbles. The rough, crinkly surface of the raisins helps carbon dioxide bubbles come out of the liquid and stick to the raisins. When a raisin has enough bubbles stuck to it, they make it lighter, and up it floats. But when it reaches the surface, some of the bubbles pop. The raisin is now heavier again, and sinks. And so on ...

You can try this with other objects, too. What happens if you use a berry, a jelly bean, or a bit of chocolate instead of a raisin? What works best?

SUGAR LIGHTS

Where does light come from? The Sun, the stars, lightbulbs, flashlights, candles, and glow sticks, of course. You've probably heard of fireflies and deep-sea fish that can light up, too. Oh, and sugar lumps!

WHAT YOU'LL NEED:

★ Sugar lumps
★ Hard, sugary candies, such as mints
★ A plastic sandwich bag (self-sealing if possible)
★ Pliers
★ A very dark place

⚠ ASK AN ADULT!

1. Put a few sugar lumps and candies into the sandwich bag, and seal it up or tie it closed. This is to make sure you don't spill sugar everywhere.

2. Go into your dark place. It could be a dark room at night, or just make a dark den under a blanket.

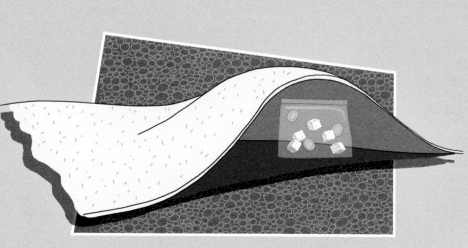

3. Ask an adult to use the pliers, as they can nip your fingers. In the dark, get the adult to hold the pliers around a candy or sugar lump (through the bag, with the sugar and candies inside).

4. Watch carefully as the adult squeezes the pliers to crush the candy or sugar lump as fast as possible. If it's dark enough, you should see a glow of light.

HOW DOES IT WORK?

This strange light is called triboluminescence. It's made by some materials when they are crushed, squeezed, or ripped apart. Scientists aren't really sure why!

There are more ways to make triboluminescence. **TRY THESE!**

▪ Rip open a self-seal envelope.
▪ Stick two strips of clear tape or packing tape together, then rip them apart as fast as possible.
▪ Get two rose quartz crystals and rub them together.
▪ Ask an adult to put some sugar lumps in a food processor, and blend them.

THE BOUNCY EGG

Take a perfectly normal, raw egg, and turn it into a bouncy rubber ball (well, an egg-shaped ball!) with this bizarre experiment.

WHAT YOU'LL NEED:

* ✴ A raw egg
* ✴ White vinegar
* ✴ A small jar or food container (big enough for the egg) with a lid
* ✴ A larger container or bowl
* ✴ A plate

1. Take your egg and gently put it into the small container. Pour in white vinegar until it completely covers the egg. Put the lid on and press or screw it down firmly.

The large container is to catch any vinegar that may leak out, as it's pretty smelly.

2. Now take the container with the egg inside, and put in into the larger container or bowl. Leave your egg to soak for at least 24 hours. You can look at it every so often to see what it's doing, but avoid picking it up or poking it.

An egg's shell contains a material called calcium carbonate, which makes it hard. Vinegar reacts with calcium carbonate and makes it dissolve away, leaving the inner part, which is a stretchy skin or "membrane." It can still hold the raw egg in, though it's not as strong—and it can bounce.

3. When the time is up, take off the lid and carefully take the egg out. It will have strange bits of "skin" on it—gently wash them off under a tap.

4. The egg should feel strangely soft and rubbery. Drop it onto the plate from a few inches up in the air, and it should bounce!

Do this really carefully, as the egg inside is still raw, and it may splat open. The person who splats it has to clean it up!

THE VANISHING GLASS

Want to know how to make a normal, everyday drinking glass disappear before your very eyes? Amaze your friends or parents with some mysterious science magic!

WHAT YOU'LL NEED:

* A small, plain, clear drinking glass
* A clear mixing bowl, big enough for the glass to fit right inside
* A large bottle of sunflower oil (the kind used for cooking)

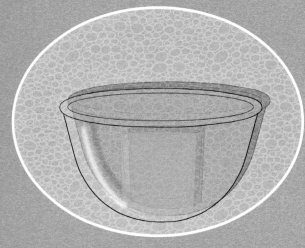

1. Make sure the glass and the bowl are clean and dry. Stand the glass inside the bowl.

2. Pour some oil into the bowl, so that it comes halfway up the glass. Pour some into the glass, too, so that it comes up to the same level.

If it doesn't work very well, try another glass. There are different types of glass, so some might match the oil better than others.

3. Look through the side of the bowl. What's happened to the bottom of the glass? If your experiment is working, it will have vanished!

4. Keep pouring more oil into the bowl, until the glass is completely submerged. Ta-daaa—it disappears!

HOW DOES IT WORK?

Glass is see-through, but you can still see it, can't you? That's because of the way light bends, or "refracts," when it shines through different materials. When you look at a glass, you can see the edges because the refraction makes you see darker and lighter areas in the glass. However, the amount of refraction that happens in oil is roughly the same as for glass. So when the oil surrounds the glass, light passes straight through the glass, and you can't see it!

THE MIGHTY STRAW

Try to stick a straw into a potato and you'll have trouble. Or your friends will ... you won't, because you know the secret! In fact, you might be able to stick it all the way through ...

WHAT YOU'LL NEED:
* ✹ A medium-sized raw potato
* ✹ Plastic drinking straws

Bendy straws won't work for this experiment. If you only have bendy straws, cut the ends off neatly, just below the bendy part.

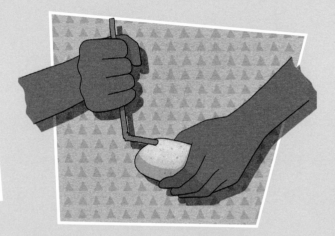

1. First, try to stick a straw into a potato. It has to be a raw one—no cheating with cooked potatoes! It's very difficult, because the potato is hard and the straw bends and crumples.

2. To make it work, you have to hold the straw in your fist, and put your thumb over the open end, like this. Don't squeeze it too hard, but hold it firmly.

3. Hold the potato in the other hand, but don't have your hand right underneath it. If the straw goes all the way through, you don't want it to stick into your hand as well!

4. Now lift up the hand holding the straw, and quickly and firmly jab it into the potato. You'll be amazed to find it really does go right in!

HOW DOES IT WORK?

It's all about the air inside the straw. When you don't have your thumb over the end, the straw is quite weak, as it only has thin walls, and crumples easily. But with your thumb over the end, the air in the straw gets stuck inside. It makes the straw stiffer and stronger, so it works more like a strong, solid stick.

BLAST THAT BALL

If you blast a ball with a blow-dryer, it will fly away across the room, won't it? Nope! Try this experiment ... and prepare to be blown away!

WHAT YOU'LL NEED:

* A blow-dryer (with a "cool" setting)
* A table tennis ball
* A tube from the inside of a kitchen roll

2. If you carefully tilt the blow-dryer, the ball should stay suspended in the air even though it's no longer directly above the dryer.

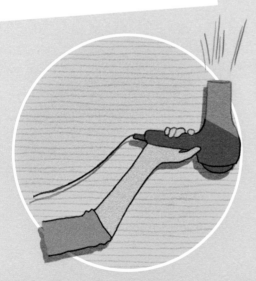

1. Turn the blow-dryer on to its "cool" setting, and tilt it so the air is blasting upward. Carefully place the table tennis ball in the jet of air around 12 inches (30cm) above the dryer. It should stay hanging in the air.

See what other lightweight objects you can keep in the air using the dryer. Try pieces of newspaper. What's the biggest piece you can keep airborne?

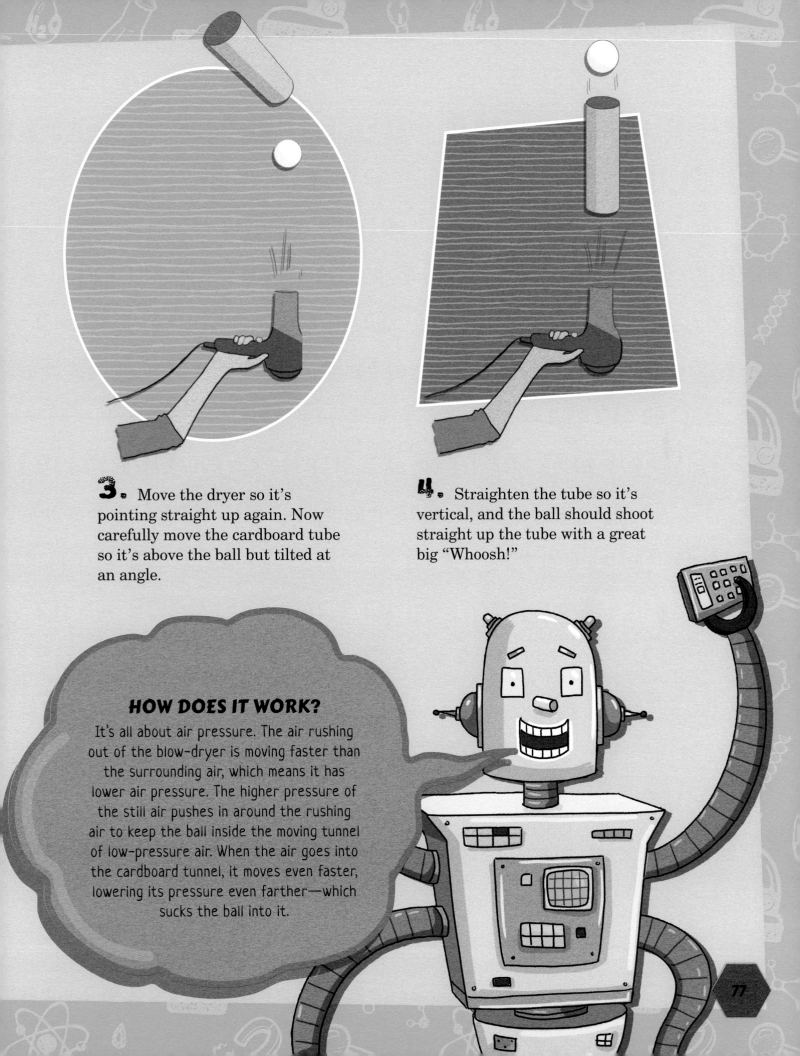

3. Move the dryer so it's pointing straight up again. Now carefully move the cardboard tube so it's above the ball but tilted at an angle.

4. Straighten the tube so it's vertical, and the ball should shoot straight up the tube with a great big "Whoosh!"

HOW DOES IT WORK?

It's all about air pressure. The air rushing out of the blow-dryer is moving faster than the surrounding air, which means it has lower air pressure. The higher pressure of the still air pushes in around the rushing air to keep the ball inside the moving tunnel of low-pressure air. When the air goes into the cardboard tunnel, it moves even faster, lowering its pressure even farther—which sucks the ball into it.

FLOWERS AND STARS

Make the flowers bloom and the stars come out with this brilliantly simple paper experiment. All you need to make it work is water.

WHAT YOU'LL NEED:
* Paper
* Colored pencils or crayons
* Scissors
* A large, shallow plate or container

1. Draw flower and star shapes on the paper. They should each have a circle in the middle, and petals or points around the edge, like these ones.

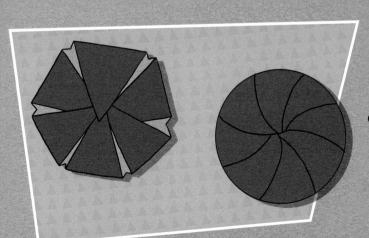

2. Cut out your flower and star shapes, and, if you like, decorate and color them in. Then fold all the petals or points inward, so that they cover the middle.

3. Put your container or plate on a flat surface, and fill it with water almost to the top. Now drop your stars and flowers in, folded side upward.

You can take the flowers and stars out, leave them to dry, and use them over and over again.

HOW DOES IT WORK?

Paper is a porous substance, which means it is full of tiny spaces that can soak up water. As water soaks into the paper, it makes it swell and get thicker. When the paper is thicker, it's hard for the folds to stay shut, and they quickly get pushed open.

For a fancier version, make one larger star or flower, and one smaller one. Stick the smaller one inside the bigger one, and fold them both up. The larger, outside one will open first, and the inside one will open more slowly, as it takes longer for the water to reach it.

EGG IN A BOTTLE

This experiment is great for amazing a crowd of people. They'll get to see an egg being sucked right inside a glass bottle by the sheer power of science.

WHAT YOU'LL NEED:

* A glass bottle with a wide opening, about 1½ inches (3cm) across
* An egg that's just slightly wider than the opening of your bottle
* A pan
* A stove
* A sink
* Cooking oil
* Matches

(!) ASK AN ADULT!

1. Ask an adult to hard-boil your egg by boiling it in a pan of water for 10 minutes, then cool it in cold water. When it's cool, carefully peel off the shell, and rinse the egg.

The type of wide-topped bottle you need is sometimes used for juice, iced tea, or chopped tomatoes. An old-fashioned glass milk bottle will also work well.

2. Make sure your glass bottle is clean and dry. Use your finger to smear a little cooking oil around the neck and top of the bottle.

3. Sit the egg in the top of the bottle to check that it is too big to fall in. Then put it to one side, within easy reach (if it does fall in, take it out and try again with a larger egg).

For the egg, if you get a "mixed sizes" box of eggs, you should find one that's just right.

4. Ask an adult to light a match, wait a second or two, then drop it into the bottle. Quickly put the egg on top of the bottle, and it should start being pulled down inside.

5. It should take just a couple of seconds for the egg to be completely sucked inside the bottle.

HOW DOES IT WORK?

Air expands as it gets hotter, and shrinks as it gets cooler. The flame heats up the air in the bottle making it expand. With the egg on top, the match goes out, and the air starts to cool and shrink, reducing the pressure in the bottle. The air pressure on the outside is higher, so it pushes down on the egg, and forces it inside.

INVISIBLE SNUFFER

With this experiment, you can put out a candle flame without touching it or blowing it. Instead, it gets snuffed out by a mysterious stream of something invisible!

WHAT YOU'LL NEED:

★ A small pitcher

★ White vinegar

★ Baking soda (sometimes known as bicarbonate of soda)

★ A teaspoon

★ A candle, holder, and matches

⚠ ASK AN ADULT!

1. First, ask an adult to put the candle in its holder, and light it with a match. Stand it somewhere safe, and put the pitcher near to it, but not too close—about 12 inches (30cm) away.

2. Pour some vinegar into the pitcher until it's about 2 inches (4cm) deep. Then take a heaped teaspoon of baking soda, and stir it into the vinegar. It will foam and bubble.

3. Now ask an adult to quickly pick up the pitcher, and tilt it carefully over the candle, as if pouring water onto the flame. They must tip it only slightly, so that no liquid or foam gets out.

4. If it works, the candle flame will flicker and go out.

HOW DOES IT WORK?

As you've seen with other experiments in this book, when vinegar and baking soda react together, they make a gas, carbon dioxide. Carbon dioxide is heavier than air, which means you can "pour" it out of a jug and it will flow downward. The candle flame needs oxygen from the air to keep burning. But the carbon dioxide gas pushes the air out of the way, so the candle goes out.

Some types of fire extinguishers contain carbon dioxide gas.

UNBELIEVABLE FORKS

Find out how to make two forks balance in a way that REALLY looks as if it shouldn't be possible. It is possible, though, thanks to the laws of balancing, but it will take a lot of practice to get right.

WHAT YOU'LL NEED:
* Two matching forks (ideally not very precious ones)
* Two cocktail sticks, toothpicks, or similar-length pieces of wooden skewers
* A lot of patience!

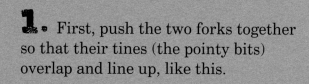

1. First, push the two forks together so that their tines (the pointy bits) overlap and line up, like this.

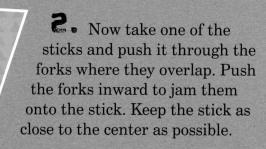

2. Now take one of the sticks and push it through the forks where they overlap. Push the forks inward to jam them onto the stick. Keep the stick as close to the center as possible.

3. Once the stick is jammed in, you should be able to find a point on the stick where it will balance on your finger.

This can be done, but it's tricky, and it may take some time to get the stick in exactly the right place and find the balancing point. Keep trying! If you find it too difficult, ask an adult to see if they can do it.

4. Take the other stick, and hold it point-upward. Now try to balance the stick with the forks on it on the very tip of the point. When you manage it— quick! Get someone to take a photo!

HOW DOES IT WORK?

An object balances on its "center of mass." That means the point that has an equal amount of weight all around it. For example, to balance a simple-shaped object like a plate on your finger, you'd put your finger right in the middle. The forks and toothpick make a much more complicated shape. It looks strange when it's balancing, but the center of mass really is near the end of the stick. That's because the handles of the forks reach back behind the stick, and spread the weight out.

HOT AND COLD EXPERIMENTS

Heat and cold affect us humans all the time, as we feel them through our skin. In fact, heat and cold have a big effect on everything else, too. Try these experiments to see how!

What is heat?

To us, heat feels pleasantly warm, or painfully scorching, while cold feels cooling, or bitterly sharp. But our experience of heat and cold are caused by just one simple thing—movement.

All matter—the stuff that everything is made of—is made up of tiny atoms, or groups of atoms called molecules. Whether they're in a solid, a liquid, or a gas, they are always moving.

When things get hotter, their atoms and molecules get more energy, and move faster. The hotter things are, the more the molecules move. Heat is simply made of movement. Cold is the opposite—there's less energy, and less movement.

Heat can spread from one thing to another as the movement is passed on. That's why putting your feet on a cozy hot water bottle warms them up!

Changes of state

Heat and cold can also make things change between a solid, a liquid, and a gas. For example, when puddles get really cold they freeze solid. Washing dries quickly in the sun, as the water turns into water vapor, a gas, and floats away. Chocolate melts from a solid to a liquid in your mouth, or when held in your hand.

Hot air, cold air

Try this simple experiment to see what happens to air as it heats up and cools down. You'll need an empty plastic bottle, a balloon, a bowl of water with ice cubes in it, and a bowl of very hot water (ask an adult to get this ready for you).

First, blow up the balloon and let it go down, then stretch it over the top of the bottle. Stand the bottle in the hot water, and hold it there for a few minutes. What happens?

Then move the bottle to the bowl with ice in it, and hold it there. What does the balloon do now?

HOW DOES IT WORK?

The bottle is full of air, which is made of gas. The air's molecules are always zooming around and crashing into each other. When the hot water heats the air, the molecules speed up. They push against each other more, and this makes them spread out and take up more space. So the air expands (gets bigger) and starts to inflate the balloon.

WATCH OUT!

These extreme experiments involve candles, hot water, hot ovens, and freezing ice. Take care when you're experimenting, and have an adult handy to do anything that involves a lot of heat.

HYDROTHERMAL VENT

At the bottom of deep oceans, there are hydrothermal vents, where hot water full of dissolved minerals comes shooting out from under the sea bed. This experiment has the same effect—but how?

WHAT YOU'LL NEED:

* ✸ A small empty glass bottle, such as a food coloring bottle
* ✸ String
* ✸ Scissors
* ✸ Hot and cold water
* ✸ Liquid food coloring
* ✸ A large plastic container or bowl
* ✸ A pitcher

⚠ ASK AN ADULT!

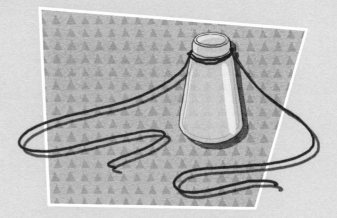

1. Cut a piece of string about 2 feet (50cm) long. Tie the middle of the string around the neck of the bottle, leaving the two long ends free.

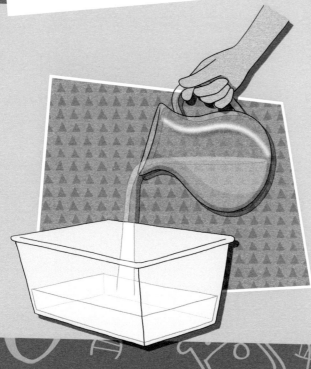

2. Stand your large bowl or container on a table, and use the pitcher to fill it with cold water.

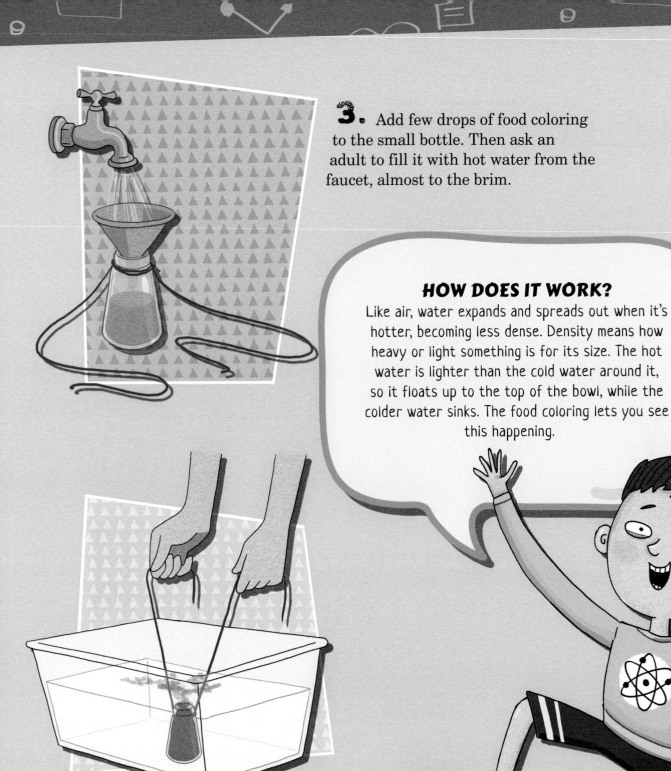

3. Add few drops of food coloring to the small bottle. Then ask an adult to fill it with hot water from the faucet, almost to the brim.

HOW DOES IT WORK?

Like air, water expands and spreads out when it's hotter, becoming less dense. Density means how heavy or light something is for its size. The hot water is lighter than the cold water around it, so it floats up to the top of the bowl, while the colder water sinks. The food coloring lets you see this happening.

4. Hold the string handles and quickly lower the bottle into the container or bowl of cold water, so that it stands on the bottom. What happens?

SPEED IT UP!

Want your chemical reaction to go faster? Just make it hotter! This simple experiment is a brilliant demonstration of how heat speeds up reactions.

WHAT YOU'LL NEED:

* Two tall, narrow glasses or jars
* A tray
* Two small bowls or cups
* Baking soda (sometimes known as bicarbonate of soda)
* White vinegar
* A teaspoon
* A tablespoon
* Hot and cold water

⊙ ASK AN ADULT!

1. Stand your two tall glasses on the tray, side by side. Carefully measure three level teaspoons of baking soda into each glass. The amounts must be exactly the same.

Make a "level" spoonful by filling the spoon, then scraping off the top with a knife so that the powder lies flat.

2. Take your two bowls, and measure out two tablespoons of vinegar into each. Then add two tablespoons of cold water to one of the bowls.

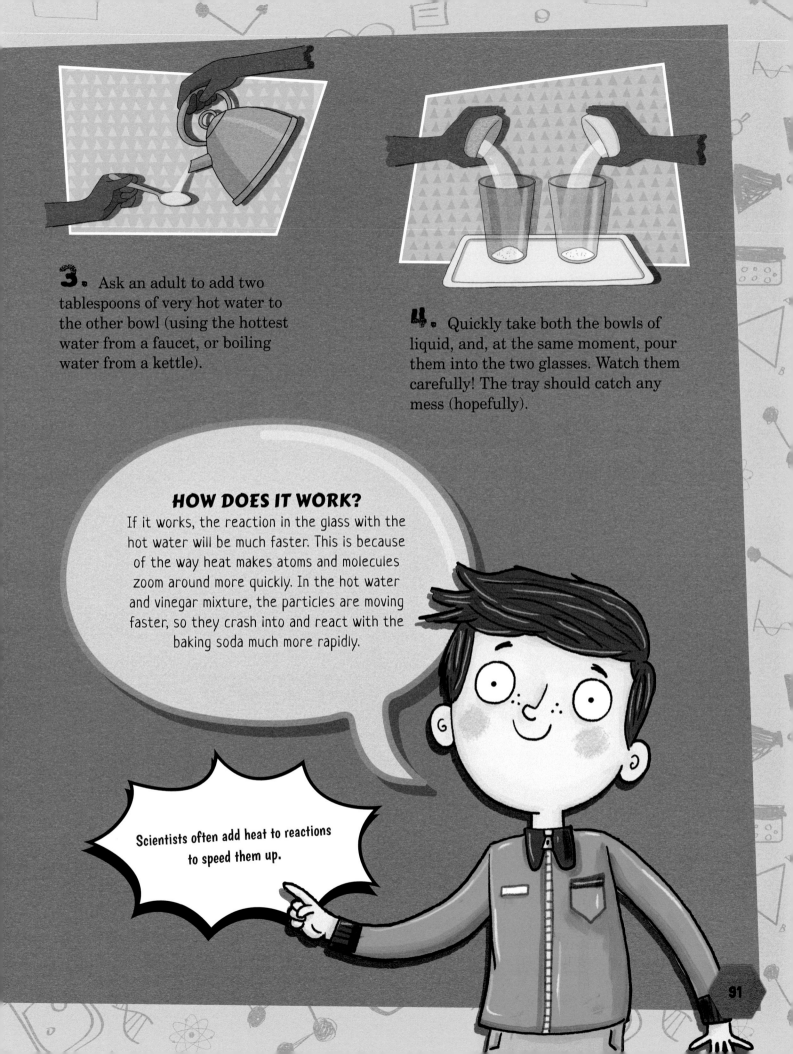

3. Ask an adult to add two tablespoons of very hot water to the other bowl (using the hottest water from a faucet, or boiling water from a kettle).

4. Quickly take both the bowls of liquid, and, at the same moment, pour them into the two glasses. Watch them carefully! The tray should catch any mess (hopefully).

HOW DOES IT WORK?

If it works, the reaction in the glass with the hot water will be much faster. This is because of the way heat makes atoms and molecules zoom around more quickly. In the hot water and vinegar mixture, the particles are moving faster, so they crash into and react with the baking soda much more rapidly.

Scientists often add heat to reactions to speed them up.

FROZEN BUBBLES

Bubbles are made of an incredibly thin layer of soapy water. So, before long, they pop! But, using extreme cold, it is possible to freeze a bubble hard. You can do this outdoors on a super-cold day, or with a freezer.

WHAT YOU'LL NEED:

* Bubble mixture and wand
* A very cold day—the temerature must be below −25°F (−5°C)—or a freezer
* A small plate and a straw (if using a freezer)

The outdoor method

1. This is quite simple, but you'll need a really cold day, well below freezing. Take your bubble mixture outside (wrap up warm!), and carefully blow a large bubble. Hold the bubble on the wand, and watch it closely as it starts to freeze.

2. When your bubble has frozen solid, try touching and squeezing it. Does it break, bend, or shatter?

The freezer method

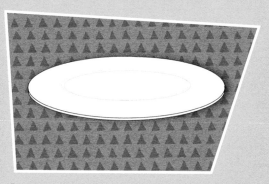

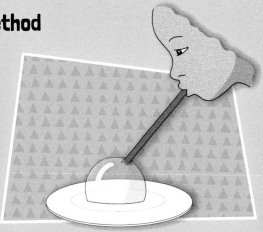

1. First, make some space in your freezer so that your plate can fit inside. Put the plate on a table and pour a drop of bubble mixture onto it.

2. Dip your straw in the bubble mixture and blow a bubble into the mixture. The bubble should spread out onto the plate.

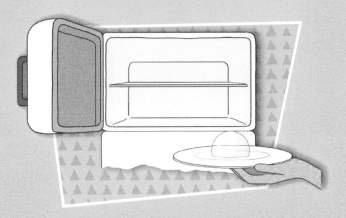

3. Quickly but carefully put the plate in the freezer, and gently close the door. Leave it for at least 10 minutes.

You may be able to see patterns of ice crystals that have formed in the bubble.

4. Take the plate out and see if you have a frozen bubble! (It may take a few attempts to get the bubble to freeze without popping.)

HOW DOES IT WORK?

It usually takes water a long time to freeze solid, for example in a pond. But the skin of a bubble is so thin—it only contains a tiny amount of water and soap—that it doesn't take long for the icy cold air to freeze it. The ice forms bit by bit, and spreads across the surface of the bubble.

UNDERWATER CANDLE

Can a candle really burn underwater? Well ... kind of! This experiment uses both heat and cold to give a candle flame an underwater home.

WHAT YOU'LL NEED:

* ★ A cylinder-shaped pillar candle
* ★ A large glass or metal bowl that's deeper than the candle
* ★ Poster putty
* ★ A pitcher
* ★ Matches
* ★ Water
* ⚠ ASK AN ADULT!

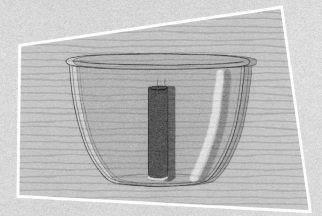

1. Roll a ball of poster putty about ½ inch (2cm) across, and stick it to the base of the candle. Press the candle hard into the bottom of the bowl, so that it stands upright and stays in place.

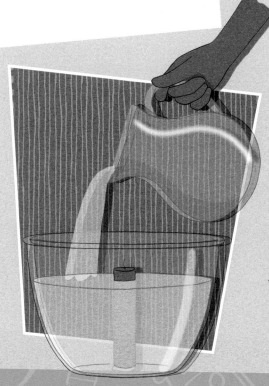

2. Stand the bowl somewhere safe and well away from other objects. Use the pitcher to fill the bowl with cold water, until the water level is about ¼ inch (1cm) below the candle's wick.

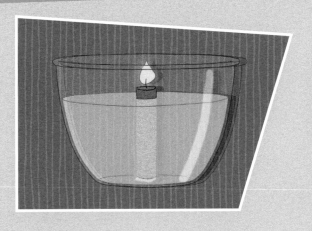

3. Once the water is calm, ask the adult to light the candle. Leave it burning, but make sure there is always an adult in the room to keep an eye on it.

4. The candle will start to burn down. But instead of going out, the flame should get lower and lower, inside a wall of wax that keeps the water out.

How far below the water level will it go? Can you take a photo from the side, showing the flame rising out of the water?

HOW DOES IT WORK?

When you light a candle, it starts burning down, using up the wax. The heat usually melts some of the wax, too, and it drips down the sides. In the water, the sides of the candle don't melt so much, because the water around them is keeping them cool. Only the wax in the middle burns down, so the flame gets lower and lower—until it's under the water surface!

PEA AND SPOON RACE

Not an egg and spoon race, but a pea and spoon race! But you don't have to run anywhere—in this experiment, heat is trying to win the race.

WHAT YOU'LL NEED:

★ Three spoons—one wooden, one metal, and one plastic, as similar in size and shape as possible.

★ Three peas, all the same size (not frozen)

★ Soft butter

★ A heatproof glass or coffee mug

★ Very hot water

⚠ ASK AN ADULT!

1. First, make sure your spoons are clean, dry, and cold, not warm.

If you don't have peas, you can use small, round candies, berries, or beads, or anything of a similar shape.

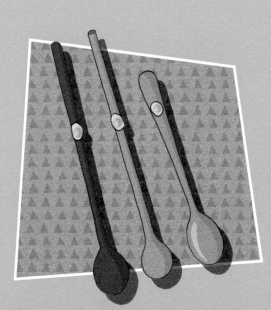

2. Use a dab of butter to stick a pea to each spoon handle. If the spoons are different lengths, line them up, and put the pea the same distance away from the round end on each one, like this.

96

3. Ask an adult to half-fill the glass with hot water from the faucet. Stand all three spoons in the water, all at the same time. Make them lean away so that their handles are not directly above the water.

4. The race is on! Heat will spread up from the water through the spoon handles. When each spoon handle gets warm, the butter will melt, and the pea will drop off. Which do you think will be first?

HOW DOES IT WORK?
When heat spreads through an object, it's called heat conduction. Some materials are much better at conducting heat than others. For example, metals are good conductors, and heat spreads through them quickly. Wood and plastic don't conduct heat as well.

Heat conduction is one reason we use different materials for different jobs. For example, a pan is made of metal to conduct heat to the food inside, but the handle may be wooden or plastic, so that it doesn't get too hot to touch.

HEATPROOF BALLOON

Can you hold a balloon in a candle flame without it popping? Of course not! Well, actually, you can, with this extreme experiment.

WHAT YOU'LL NEED:

* Two balloons
* A candle and candle holder
* Matches
* Water

(!) **ASK AN ADULT!**

Do this experiment in the kitchen or bathroom, just in case it goes wrong and you get water everywhere!

1. First, do a test to check that candles really do make balloons pop. Ask an adult to put the candle in its holder in a safe place, and light it. Blow up the first balloon, tie it closed, and ask the adult to hold it over the candle so that it just touches the flame. Pop!

2. Now take the second balloon, and put some cold water inside it. The easiest way to do this is to stretch the opening of the balloon over the end of a faucet. You only need to fill it about a quarter full, then blow it up to full size the normal way.

3. Tie the balloon closed, and dry any water drops off the outside of it. Now ask your adult to carefully hold the balloon over the candle flame, like before.

4. If it works, it should be possible to hold the balloon in the flame for a few seconds, without it popping.

HOW DOES IT WORK?

When the hot flame touches the balloon rubber, it gets so hot that it immediately melts, and the balloon pops. But when there's water in the balloon, the heat from the flame mostly goes into the cold water. It takes a lot of heat energy to warm up water, so it stays cool for a while, and keeps the balloon skin cool, too—even though there's a flame touching it!

MELTING WITHOUT HEAT

Set your friends or family this ice-fishing challenge, and see if they can do it. It seems impossible, until you know the secret!

WHAT YOU'LL NEED:
* A glass
* A tray
* Water
* Ice cubes
* String
* Scissors
* Salt

1. First, fill the glass to the top with cold water, and stand it on the tray (to catch any spills). Put an ice cube in the water.

2. Cut a piece of string about 12 inches (30cm) long. Now challenge someone to use the string to pick up the ice cube. They can only touch the ice cube with the string, not with their hands, and they can't use a spoon or any other tools.

3. Do they give up? Here's how it's done. Take the salt and sprinkle some onto the ice cube.

4. Carefully lay the string across the top of the salty ice cube, and leave it hanging there for a minute.

5. Now pick up the two ends of the string. The ice cube should be stuck to the string, so you can easily lift it out of the glass.

HOW DOES IT WORK?

Water freezes at a temperature of 32°F (0°C). But salty water has a freezing point that's several degrees lower. So when you add salt to the ice cube, it starts to melt. The string sinks into the melted water. However, melting ice takes heat out of the water, and it gets colder. Cold enough to freeze again! The water refreezes around the string, sticking it to the ice

This is why we sometimes put salt on icy roads and sidewalks. As it lowers the melting point of water, it makes the ice melt (as long as the weather's not too cold).

SHRINKING CHIP PACKET

Make a perfectly normal potato chip packet into a cute tiny weeny chip packet! All it takes is a bit of easy baking.

WHAT YOU'LL NEED:

* An empty potato chip bag (plastic, not foil)
* Baking, greaseproof, or wax paper
* A baking tray
* An oven
* Oven mitts
* A dish towel

⚠ ASK AN ADULT!

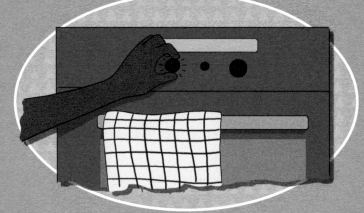

1. First, give your potato chip packet a good wash inside, and dry it completely. Ask an adult to turn the oven on and heat it to about 350°F (180°C or gas mark 4).

2. Take a large piece of wax paper and put your bag on it. Smooth the bag flat.

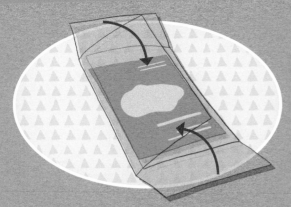

3. Fold the wax paper over the bag on the left- and right-hand sides. Then fold over at the top and bottom to make a simple parcel.

HOW DOES IT WORK?

Most things expand or get bigger when they're heated—so what's going on? A potato chip bag is made of a polymer plastic, which is made of chains of molecules. When they are heated, the chains pull together and tighten up, making the packet smaller, thicker, and harder.

4. Turn the parcel over and put it on the baking sheet. Ask an adult to put it in the oven. Bake the bag for about 7 minutes. Ask an adult to check it every couple of minutes.

5. When you can see that the packet has shrunk inside the parcel, ask the adult to take the baking sheet out of the oven and put it on a heatproof surface. They should then fold up the dish towel and use it to press down on the parcel to flatten the chip bag.

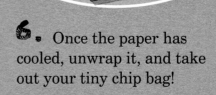

6. Once the paper has cooled, unwrap it, and take out your tiny chip bag!

HOT AIR BALLOON

Hot air balloons were the first flying machines ever invented. This one isn't big enough to carry a person, but it might carry a tiny paper figure.

WHAT YOU'LL NEED:

* A very large, thin plastic bag—a dry cleaning bag is perfect
* Thin string or sewing thread
* Clear tape
* A small, clean yogurt pot to act as a basket
* A blow-dryer
* At least one other person to help

⊘ ASK AN ADULT!

1. Lay the plastic bag on the floor with the open end toward you. Cut four pieces of string, each about 8 inches (20cm) long, and lay them next to the bag, ready.

2. Use small pieces of tape to attach the four pieces of string to the open end of the bag, equally spaced around the opening.

3. Tape the other ends of the strings to the sides of the yogurt pot. You should be able to hold the bag up so that the basket hangs down below it.

Check to see if your bag has any small holes in it. If it does, patch them with tiny pieces of tape.

4. Hold the balloon up while an adult uses a blow-dryer to blow hot air into the open end at the bottom. Keep holding the balloon as it fills up with hot air.

5. When the balloon seems to be pulling upward, let it go. If it works, it should fly up into the air, for just a little while—until it cools and comes back down.

HOW DOES IT WORK?

The hot air from the blow-dryer is less dense and lighter than the cooler air around the balloon. This makes the balloon lighter than air, so it floats upward. It will work best in cool air—so if you have no luck indoors, you could try this in a garage or yard, if it's colder there.

CRUSH THE CAN

Crush a can in a split second using just the power of air pressure!
Warning: this experiment is VERY hot, so make sure an adult does it.

WHAT YOU'LL NEED:

* ★ A large container, like a bucket or dishwashing bowl
* ★ Cold water
* ★ Lots of ice cubes
* ★ An empty drinks can
* ★ A teaspoon
* ★ A stove—a portable one is best so you can do the experiment outside
* ★ A pair of long metal tongs, such as barbecue tongs
* ★ An oven mitt
* ⚠ ASK AN ADULT!

1. Put the bucket or bowl near the stove. Fill it about two-thirds full with cold water, and add ice cubes to make it even colder.

2. Put a teaspoon of water into the can. Ask the adult to switch on the stove. The adult should then wear the oven mitt and hold the can firmly in the tongs.

3. If it's an electric stove, the adult can stand the can directly on the stove once it's red hot. If it's a gas stove, the adult should hold the can over the flame instead.

4. Let the can heat up until the water inside boils, and steam comes out of the hole. Make sure everyone is standing well back!

5. The adult should then use the tongs to turn the can upside down, and quickly plunge it into the icy water. What happens?

The layer of air around the Earth is always squeezing and pressing on us, just as it did on the can. We don't feel it because we're used to it, and our bodies are built to resist it.

HOW DOES IT WORK?

When you heat up the can, the air inside it gets very hot. It expands, and most of it gets pushed out of the can. When the can hits the cold water, the air inside suddenly cools and shrinks. But air can't rush back into the can because the water is blocking it. Instead, the low pressure inside the can, and the high pressure of the air and water around the can, squeezes the can and crushes it.

LIVING EXPERIMENTS

Studying living things is a huge part of science. Life is all around us—trees, grass, germs, pets, farm animals, and wildlife—and we ourselves are alive, too! Living things, including the human body, work in all kinds of amazing ways.

WHAT IS LIFE?

So what makes something alive? Here's a list of things that all living things do. If it doesn't do all these things, it's not alive!

Move
Respond to its environment (though some other things move, too, such as waves or clouds).

Grow
Start off smaller and get bigger.

Respire
Make energy from food, usually using gases from the air.

Eat
Take in food of some kind.

Sense
Detect things around it, using its senses.

Reproduce
Make copies of itself—by having babies, for example.

Excrete
Let out waste. For example, there are waste gases in the breath you breathe out.

Hands in the air

Try this quick and easy experiment to show how blood carries oxygen to your muscles. You need two arms, two hands, and a timer.

Set the timer going, then put one arm straight up in the air, and the other down by your side. Start opening and closing both your hands as fast as you can, making a star shape, then a fist, and repeating.

How long can you keep this going? As time goes on, do your hands start to feel different from each other? Can you keep them both moving at the same speed—or do you have to stop moving one a bit sooner than the other?

HOW DOES IT WORK?

Muscle cells use oxygen to make energy, so that your body can move. Sticking your hand up makes it hard for enough blood to get uphill to the muscles to deliver the oxygen needed to keep the hand moving. When the muscles run short of oxygen, they release a chemical called lactic acid to help them make energy—but this only works for a while, and is quite painful. So your hand hurts and wants to stop moving. The other hand is still getting lots of blood, so it can keep going!

SEEDS ON A SOCK

Look at the Earth from space, and you'll see a LOT of green. It's all the plants! Plants can spread over large areas using seeds, which can get carried long distances by wind, water, or animals. And that includes you!

WHAT YOU'LL NEED:

* A large, old, unwanted sock
* Somewhere wild to go for a walk, such as a woodland, hill, or park
* Scissors
* An old cardboard box, such as a shoebox
* Potting compost (from a garden center or supermarket)

! ASK AN ADULT!

1. First, get an adult to agree to take you for a walk, somewhere with lots of plants. Before you set off, pull an old sock over one of your shoes. An adult's sock is best, as it will fit over your shoe more easily.

You'll probably get the best results in summer or fall, when plants are making the most seeds.

2. Go for your walk with the sock on. When you get home, take the sock off, and use the scissors to cut along one side, so that it opens out flat.

3. Put a shallow layer of compost in the bottom of your box, then lay the opened-out sock on top, muddy side up.

4. Cover it with another layer of compost, and then sprinkle it with water.

HOW DOES IT WORK?

Seeds have to find ways of getting to other places to grow. They may be blown by the wind, or stick to passing animals. Your sock is a bit like animal fur, so seeds will stick to it. If you then give them soil, water, and sunlight, they'll start to grow.

5. Put the box somewhere sunny and warm, such as a south-facing windowsill, for a week or two. Water it a little every day. With luck, you'll see several different plants starting to grow.

You could also try doing this experiment when you're on vacation to see if you get different plants.

STICKY SLIME

Snails and slugs leave silvery, slimy trails wherever they go. Have you ever wondered what that slimy stuff is, and what's it for? This is an experiment to try in a park or garden in spring or summer.

WHAT YOU'LL NEED:
* A plastic tray or large plastic plate
* A snail and a slug (most yards have plenty)
* Lettuce, apple, or cucumber as food
* 2 paper clips
* 2 small coins

You can pick slugs and snails up with your fingers, as long as you wash your hands afterward. But if you don't want to touch them, you could wear rubber gloves.

1. First, find some snails and slugs. Look around plants and under leaves. They especially like vegetable plants. If you can't find a slug and a snail, just one of them will do. Be sure to handle them gently.

2. Put your slug and snail at one side of your tray or plate. Encourage them to move across it by placing food in front of them (it could take a while!).

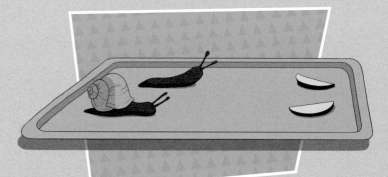

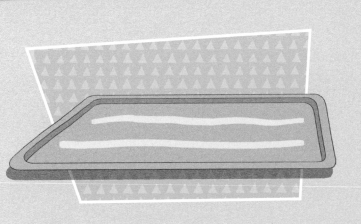

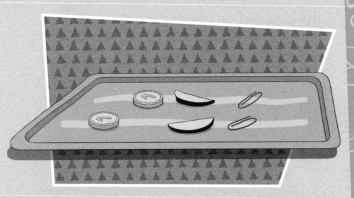

3. Put the slug and snail back where you found them. Now test their slime. Do the two trails look different from each other?

4. Try sticking a piece of food, a paper clip, and a coin to each slime trail, then slowly turning the tray or plate upside down to see if they stay on. How sticky is the slime? Is one trail stickier than the other?

A plain plate or tray, with no patterns, will make it easier to see the slime!

HOW DOES IT WORK?

Snail and slug slime is a gel made of a stringy substance mixed with other chemicals. It lets snails and slugs glide more easily over rough surfaces. It's also very sticky, helping them to slither up plant stems, walls, and flowerpots. And it kills germs and protects the snail or slug's skin—which is why it's sometimes used to make beauty creams!

PAVLOV'S PETS

Russian scientist, Ivan Pavlov, did a famous experiment on dogs to study how they learn. It's easy to try at home if you have a dog or cat. Don't worry, it's harmless!

WHAT YOU'LL NEED:
* A pet dog or cat
* Their regular food
* A bell, duck squeaker, or something else that makes an unusual noise

Your bell or other noise-maker should be something the dog or cat has not heard before. If you can't find anything, an unusual smartphone alarm tone should work.

1. To do this experiment, you need your cat or dog to link the new sound with being fed. Every time they are just about to be fed, make the noise a few times. (Make sure the noise isn't too loud, or you might scare them.)

Don't make the noise at any other time except feeding time, as this could confuse your pet and the experiment won't work.

2. After a few days, make the noise just before feeding time, but without having any food ready. If it's worked, they should still come running for their food.

3. You could try more tests. Does one pet learn more quickly than another? Does it work on pet guinea pigs, hamsters, or fish? Can you link a different sound to going for a walk, or playing with a toy?

HOW DOES IT WORK?

In his experiments, Pavlov found that dogs drooled and dribbled when they saw food. He rang a bell at feeding time, and eventually the dogs would drool whenever they heard the bell, even if there was no food around. The experiment shows how animals can learn by connecting unrelated things together in their brains. If your cat or dog runs in expecting to be fed when it hears the noise, you can tell the experiment has worked.

TWO POINT TOUCH TEST

This is an experiment for you and friends or family to try on each other. You might think your skin can tell the difference between one touch and two—but it's not that simple!

WHAT YOU'LL NEED:

* Paper clips
* A ruler
* A pencil and paper
* At least two people

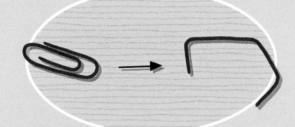

1. Open out a paper clip and bend it into a rough "U" shape, like this. The two ends should be lined up and pointing the same way.

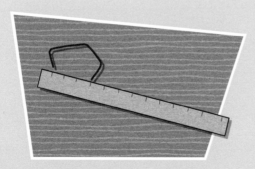

2. Use the ruler to measure the distance between the ends of the paper clip, and write it down.

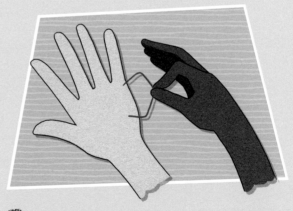

3. To do the test, the person being tested should sit down and close their eyes, while the tester uses the paperclip to gently press on their skin. Start with the palm of the hand. Ask if the person can feel one point, or two.

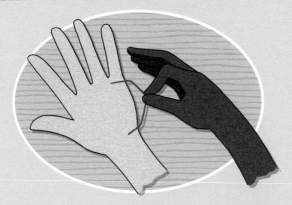

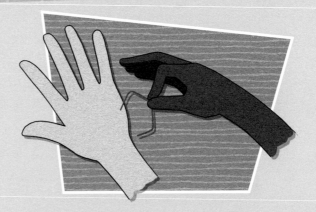

4. If they can only feel one, move the ends farther apart, measure them again, and try again. If they can feel two, move the ends closer together, and try again.

5. Sometimes, at random, just press one end of the paper clip onto the skin. This makes sure the person being tested really can tell the difference between one and two points.

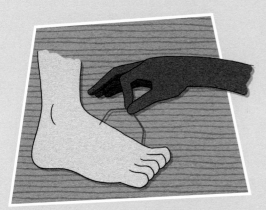

6. Repeat the experiment on these different parts of the body:
- Top of the foot
- Calf
- Fingertip
- Cheek
- Shoulder

Write down how far apart the ends of the paper clip have to be before the person can feel two points instead of one. For example, on the back of the hand, it might be a ½ inch (12mm).

HOW DOES IT WORK?

Skin isn't the same all over the body. Some areas, such as hands and fingers, are much better at feeling fine detail, and can sense two points even when they are very close together. Other areas are much less sensitive. Why do you think the hands have a better sense of touch than other areas, such as the calf?

SEEING IS BELIEVING

These amazing illusions reveal the science behind the way we see. It's not just your eyes that see, but also your brain. It tries to make sense of what your eyes detect, and sometimes gets it a bit wrong.

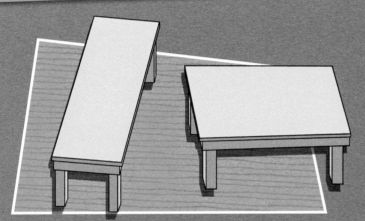

1. TABLETOPS
Which of these two tables is longer? Pretty obvious, right? Get a ruler and measure each table top's sides. You might be surprised.

Try each illusion out, and see if it works on your friends and family members too.

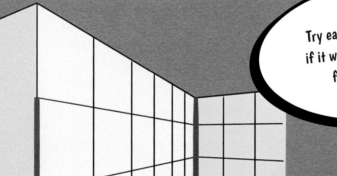

TALK TO THE THE HAND

2. LINE SIZES
This well-known illusion is called the Ponzi illusion. Which pink line is the longest, or are they the same length? Measure them and see.

3. READ THE SIGN
This one's simple—just read the sign! What does it say?

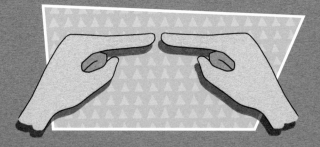

4. THE FLYING SAUSAGE

Hold your hands at arm's length, with your index fingers pointing toward each other, about ¼ inch apart, like this.

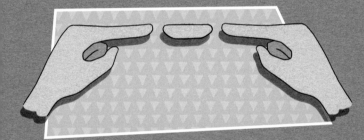

Now, look past your fingers at something far away. You should see a sausage form in mid-air between your fingertips!

5. SHADOW SHADES

Look at the two squares marked A and B. Which one is the darker shade of gray?

HOW DO THEY WORK?

1. TABLETOPS: Because your brain interprets these images as three dimensional, it sees them as long and short tables—even though the "short" one is actually longer than the "long" one.

2. LINE SIZES: The diagonal lines make you think one pink line is near and the other far away. If they were the same size, the far away one should look smaller. As it doesn't, your brain decides it must be huge, when in fact it's slightly shorter than the "near" one.

3. READ THE SIGN: Did you spot the second "the"? Many people don't! The brain is often too busy to take in every little detail. Instead, it jumps to conclusions, and assumes things make sense.

4. THE FLYING SAUSAGE: Your eyes see the world from two slightly different angles. When you focus on something, you don't notice. But when you focus far away, the two different views of your fingers overlap each other, making the strange sausage shape.

5. SHADOW SHADES: Your brain judges how light or dark something is by its surroundings, so it thinks the square in the shadow must be lighter than the other one. In fact, they're both exactly the same shade, as you can see below.

TOUCH TRICKERY

Optical illusions aren't the only kind. There are also tactile illusions, which confuse your brain about what you can feel. Try these!

Try each illusion out and test them on friends and family. You'll need a helper for some of them.

1. THE TWO-NOSE ILLUSION

Cross your first and second fingers over each other, as far as they can go. Then use them to touch and feel the tip of your nose. It feels as if you have two noses! It works with other round objects too, such as a marble.

2. THE LONG NOSE ILLUSION

For this, you need a friend who doesn't mind you touching their nose, and two chairs. Ask them to sit right in front of you. Shut your eyes, and use one hand to touch your own nose. Reach your other hand forward, and touch your friend's nose, using the exact same movements. It will feel as if their nose is yours, and your nose is really long!

3. FLOATING ARMS

Stand in a doorway, lift your arms out to your sides, and push the backs of your hands against the door frame. Keep pushing them as hard as you can for about a minute. Then step away from the doorway and relax. Your arms will seem to magically float upward!

4. SILENT CHALK

Use a piece of chalk to write or scribble on a blackboard—or, if you don't have a blackboard, a sidewalk, or patio. Then put in some earplugs or earphones playing music, or ask a friend to cover your ears. Try using the chalk again. It should feel much smoother!

HOW DO THEY WORK?

1. THE TWO-NOSE ILLUSION: It's very rare for the outside edges of your first and second fingers to be touching the same round object. The brain ignores your fingers being crossed, and instead decides that the fingers must be touching two different surfaces.

2. THE LONG NOSE ILLUSION: Your brain knows where your body parts are in space—so it knows your arm is far away from your face. But because both hands can feel a nose, it gets confused, and thinks your nose must be really long.

3. FLOATING ARMS: As the brain keeps sending the signal to lift your arms, it stops thinking about it, and starts sending the signal automatically. When you step away, the signal keeps going, even though you are not trying to lift your arms—and makes them seem to lift by themselves.

4. SILENT CHALK: The brain uses information from other senses to help it understand touch sensations. When you write with chalk, the scraping sound adds to the experience, making it feel rougher. Without the sound, it feels different!

ANT CAFE

To do this experiment, you'll need to first find an ants' nest. If you spot ants in your yard, park, or playground, you can set up this experiment close to where you've seen them.

WHAT YOU'LL NEED:

* Three sticky notes (or just use paper and clear tape)
* A ruler
* A pen
* Plain white sugar
* Brown sugar
* Artificial sweetener powder
* A teaspoon
* An ants' nest

(!) ASK AN ADULT!

1. Set up your experiment close to an ants' nest. If you can't find a nest, place it where you can see, or have seen, ants walking around or coming out of the ground.

Keep well away from the ants and don't bother them or touch them. Have an adult nearby.

2. Put the ruler on the ground and stick the three sticky notes along it. Bend them down slightly so that they lie flat against the ground.

3. Put a teaspoonful of white sugar on one note, a teaspoonful of brown sugar on another, and a teaspoonful of artificial sweetener on the third. Label each note with the type of food that is on it.

> You could use a video camera or smartphone to video the ants feeding. Speeding the video up afterward will let you see quickly where the ants spent the most time.

4. Wait and watch to see if the ants come to your cafe. Which foods do they visit the most, and which the least?

HOW DOES IT WORK?

Ants seek out high-calorie food to give them energy. Sugar has a lot of calories, so it's usually very popular with ants. They may taste the artificial sweetener, but they can tell it doesn't contain as many calories, so they prefer the real sugar. Do they prefer one type of sugar to another? If so, this may be to do with the size of the grains, and how easy the sugar is to move and eat.

THE YEAST BALLOON

Yeast is a living thing, but it's not a plant or an animal. It's a type of fungus, and is related to mushrooms and mold. This balloon experiment lets you collect the gas that yeast makes as it grows.

WHAT YOU'LL NEED:

* An empty small plastic drinks bottle
* A funnel
* Active dried yeast
* Sugar
* A teaspoon
* Hot water from the faucet
* A balloon

⚠ ASK AN ADULT!

1. Drop a teaspoon of dried yeast into the bottle, using the funnel. Then add a teaspoon of sugar, and shake the bottle around a bit to mix them together.

2. Ask an adult to add medium-hot water from the faucet to the bottle, to a depth of about 1 inch (3cm). Gently shake and swirl the bottle to mix the water in.

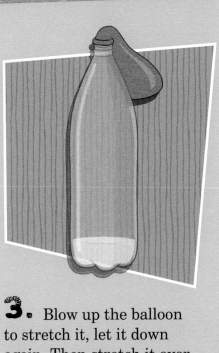

3. Blow up the balloon to stretch it, let it down again. Then stretch it over the neck of the bottle.

4. Leave the bottle in a warm place, such as a sunny windowsill or near a radiator, and watch what happens.

HOW DOES IT WORK?

Dried yeast is made up of lots of yeast cells. These are single-celled organisms that are much too small to see. When they get warm water and food (the sugar), they become "active", and start to feed and grow. As the yeast feeds on the sugar and turns it into energy, it makes bubbles of carbon dioxide gas as waste. You can see the bubbles forming in the mixture. As they pop, the gas starts to fill the bottle and the balloon.

When yeast is added to bread dough, the carbon dioxide bubbles make the dough rise and fill the bread with spaces, which makes it soft and squashy.

MEMORY TEST

Some things are easy to learn and remember, and others are much harder—people's memories don't always work very well! Try this memory test and see how well you do.

WHAT YOU'LL NEED:

* A dish towel
* A pen and paper
* A stopwatch or timer
* A tray
* At least one other person to be the tester
* A selection of ten different everyday objects, such as a key, a pen, a nail, toys, candies, a glove, a phone, a table tennis paddle, a tape measure, and so on.

1. The tester should collect all the objects together without you seeing them. They should just pick whatever objects they have to hand, and which are roughly the same size.

2. The tester should place the objects on a tray or table, and then hide them by covering them with the dish towel.

3. Now sit at the table with your pen and paper to take the test. Using the timer, the tester should remove the dish towel and show you the objects for ten seconds, before covering them up again. Then, the tester should give you one minute to write down all the objects you can remember.

4. Take off the dish towel and see how many you got right. Which ones did you remember first? Which did you forget?

HOW DOES IT WORK?

This game tests your short-term memory, which you use for storing things you've just experienced. People store memories more easily if they make them feel emotions. So, if you LOVE chocolate, you're likely to remember a chocolate bar. If you're scared of spiders, a plastic spider will stick in your brain. Look at your results and see if this was true for you.

You can test lots of different things with this experiment. For example, you could test people of different ages, and see who has the best memory. Or try testing your memory in the morning and at bedtime—when does it work best?

GLOSSARY

air pressure The force of air as it pushes on things.

atom A tiny particle that makes up everything in the Universe.

calorie A unit for measuring the amount of energy a food can provide for the body.

carbon dioxide A gas that can be used to form small bubbles in liquid (such as soda) making it fizzy.

conduction The way that heat spreads through an object.

density A measure of how compact something is and how much matter it is made of.

electricity A form of energy, made up of flowing electrons, that produces power.

electron A tiny particle, even smaller than an atom, with a negative charge.

energy The capacity to move, work, and transfer heat.

expand To increase in size.

force A push or pull on an object that causes a change in its movement.

gas A light, airlike substance that has no fixed shape.

gravity A force that tries to pull two objects together. Earth's gravity is what keeps us on the ground, and what makes objects fall.

inertia A force that keeps an object in its existing state, either moving or at rest, unless changed by an external force.

inflate To make something bigger by filling it with air.

lactic acid An acid produced by the body when exercising that can feel painful.

matter The stuff that makes up you, the world, and everything in the Universe. Matter can be a solid, liquid, or gas.

membrane A thin, flexible layer or covering.

molecule A tiny part of a substance made up of two or more atoms joined together. A molecule is the smallest unit of a substance that still behaves like that substance.

organism An individual living thing.

oxygen A gas that is essential for life.

particle A tiny piece of something.

polymer A chemical substance that is made up of long chains of molecules.

porous Containing many tiny openings through which water can pass.

pressure A force that pushes against something.

refraction When light, heat, or sound is bent when passing through a material.

respire To breathe.

rocket A flying device driven by gases being forced out of its rear.

solid A substance that has a fixed volume and shape.

static electricity Electricity that collects on the surface of something and does not flow as a current.

surface tension The force that pushes the molecules on the surface of a liquid together, making a thin layer.

vortex A whirling mass of air or water.

water vapor Water in the air in the form of a gas.